The $21 Challenge

We show you how to
feed your family with
$21 for one whole week!

Fiona Lippey and Jackie Gower

Simple **SAVINGS**

Simple Savings International Pty Ltd
PO Box 1777
Buderim QLD 4556
Australia
Website: www.21dollarchallenge.com
Email: book@21dollarchallenge.com

Published by Simple Savings International Pty Ltd 2009
Copyright © Simple Savings International Pty Ltd 2009

Reprinted 2009, 2010, 2011, 2011

Designed and typeset by Kate Andrew
Indexed by Alice Stephens

Illustrations © Steve Panozzo – www.noz.com.au

Photo credits:
  Front cover, rear cover, pages 4 and 5 © richard leonard photography dot com
  Page 10 © Minna Burgess
  Page 15 © Elise Sefton Photography
  Page 31 © Allison Hernach
  Page 33 © Michelle Cail
  Page 34 © Richard Whitby
  Page 35 © Leisa Bye
  Page 36 © Bayside Photography
  Page 41 © Deb Joyce

Printed in America by CreateSpace

ISBN-13: 978-1466369436
ISBN-10: 1466369434
LCCN: 2011918023
BISAC: Cooking / General

Introduction

The average family of four currently spends $320 a week on food. But what if you could get your food bill down to just $21 this week? In this book you will learn tips and tricks to help you slash your food bill to an all-time low.

Here is your chance to make some BIG headway, the quick way. It's time for you to claw back your money from the store and keep it where it belongs – firmly in your wallet.

You will be amazed how simple it is. Since its inception, thousands of Simple Savings members have taken the $21 Challenge with fantastic results. There are no losers in the $21 Challenge – it's a game everybody wins!

Enjoy!

Fiona and Jackie

About the Authors

Fiona Lippey

Twelve years ago, when Fiona Lippey and her now husband Matt first moved in together, they had very little money. They had $20 left to last the week and needed $10 of that money for bus fares. That left just $10 for food! However, Fiona discovered to her amazement that with a smarter way of shopping she could stretch her $10 to buy enough fruit, vegetables, groceries and meat to get the two of them through the week. It opened her eyes to a new way of life.

Time passed. Fiona and Matt got married, had a baby and were living happily on next to nothing. For six months Fiona watched other moms struggling on incomes three to four times higher than her own. It was frustrating. Fiona's background in industrial design had given her an insight into the world of sales and marketing. She could see all the tricks companies used to manipulate vulnerable new moms into parting with their money, even if they couldn't. Fiona wished there was someone out there protecting these moms from unscrupulous marketers – but there wasn't. So Fiona and Matt took matters into their own hands. They started a website to empower families and turn them into smarter shoppers. Since then, Simple Savings has evolved into a massive website averaging 11 million hits per month. Now a happy family of six, Fiona and Matt continue to run Simple Savings from their three bedroom home in sunny Queensland, where they teach 200,000 families a week how to enjoy a better life.

Jackie Gower

Jackie Gower jokingly credits her children as being triggers for her uncontrollable spending addiction. Previously sensible with money, the onset of motherhood turned Jackie into a shopping victim overnight. She wanted her kids to have EVERYTHING! Well – that was what being a good mom was all about, wasn't it? Jackie's idea of a family outing was taking her children to a department store and spending $250 on stuff. Every week.

Jackie and her husband Noel became proud home owners in 2003. Unfortunately, this only compounded the problem. She wanted to fill her new home with beautiful things and fill it she did! Unhappy in her job, shopping became an almost daily way to relieve the boredom. By the time she discovered Simple Savings in 2004, Jackie was lying awake at night worrying if she had left enough in the bank to pay the mortgage.

The day Jackie joined Simple Savings, things changed. She was so amazed at the effect the website was having on her that she asked to become part of the Simple Savings team. She began documenting her savings journey in a blog on the site, under the name Penny Wise and writes a weekly column for That's Life under the same name. Jackie and Noel live with their teenage sons on New Zealand's beautiful Coromandel Peninsula. They love living at the beach and growing their own food and enjoy nothing more than breezing down the supermarket aisles, ignoring all the things they used to buy.

Dedicated to cheeky husbands everywhere.

Contents

Contents

Part 1
What is it all about?

What exactly is the $21 Challenge? It is your ticket to saving an easy $300 in just seven days! In this book you will learn tips and tricks to help you slash hundreds off your food bill for the week.

It is a game!

The $21 Challenge is best summed up by Simple Savings member Sandra Knowles. She likes it to popular TV game show, *Survivor*.

"Pretend you have no income for one week. Now imagine you have $21 in the bank left for groceries. How are you going to survive? It's like the reality show 'Survivor', but instead of going away to some remote location you are stranded in your kitchen with only your pantry, freezer and fridge to help you. You have been given lifelines, like recipe books and the Simple Savings website. Will you win the Challenge?"

The first ever $21 Challenge

It all started when a Simple Savings member named Barbara told us about a joke her husband had played on her. Little did he know what he had started! Barb had asked her husband to bring home some grocery money and thinking it was a great laugh, he returned waving a single $20 bill. How on earth could she feed the two of them and their two teenage boys for a week on that? Determined to prove she could do it, Barb found an extra $1 bill – and the $21 Challenge was born!

The $21 Challenge today

Since that first $21 Challenge, thousands of households have taken part in the seven day grocery bill slashing marathon. Many now routinely use it to help them through tough times, cope with unexpected bills or earn family rewards faster. They have learned how to get back in charge of their finances, regain control of their life and 'find' money where they thought there was none. The Challenge teaches valuable skills which last long after the initial seven days.

In today's tough times we need all the help we can get. The $21 Challenge is something positive you can do for your household – you can see results FAST, and make a big difference to your budget.

We will show you how Barbara got through the first ever $21 Challenge week and how you can too!

Your mission

Your mission, is to do what Barb did and aim to spend only $21 to feed your household for an entire week. It can be done! All you need is a little know-how and a steel resolve. How many of us head to the supermarket to buy the same old things week after week, regardless of whether we actually need to or not? But what if you couldn't get to the store one week? Or there just wasn't enough money to go round? You'd have to make the best use of what you've got – and that's what the $21 Challenge is all about.

How you will accomplish your mission:

By sitting down with a cup of tea and soaking up this book! You will learn everything you need to know to succeed at your own $21 Challenge, including:

- how to protect yourself during uncertain economic times
- how to get out of the usual rut and boost your self esteem
- how to feel more in control of your life
- how to make a plan so you will no longer struggle from day to day trying to work out what to feed your family
- how to get the best value from the food you buy
- how to enjoy cooking (without feeling like you're chained to the kitchen!)
- how to find food when you think there is none
- how to claw back hours of free time
- how to exist without fast food
- how to feel more financially secure
- how to save money cooking food from scratch
- how to substitute ingredients instead of running to the store every five minutes
- how to raid your own house and turn clutter into nutritious meals
- how to reduce your household's ecological footprint
- how to make your life a whole lot easier!

Together we're going to whip you into the savviest shopper around!

How low can you go?

The power is in YOUR hands! Throughout this book we stress that this is a personal challenge. If you feel that $21 is too ambitious for your first attempt, adjust your goal to suit your household. You could try aiming for $21 but for main meals only, or aiming for $21 excluding bread and milk, or simply deduct $21 from your average weekly grocery bill for every person you feed. Whatever your goal, the important thing is you are saving money, having fun and improving with each Challenge. You will find as time goes on that you are capable of far more than you realize!

It's for ONE week, not EVERY week!

It's a common misconception that we expect people to live off $21 every week. Of course this is ridiculous. Trying to feed a whole family on such a small amount week-in, week-out would be pretty much impossible, or at the very least seriously bad for your health, unless you went back in time a few years and converted every inch of your yard to a vegetable garden to feed your family and livestock.

To clarify once and for all, the $21 Challenge is for one week only. It's a trump card you can pull out when, for whatever reason, you need a little extra cash to see you through a tough month. However, with a little practise people often find they can keep going for two weeks in a row, or even three. But, don't just take our word for it! Here are some success stories from Challenge families who have 'been there and done it'!

I am saving $12,000 per year!

"The $21 Challenge has really made me aware of the prices and quality of groceries. We realized we were wasteful, impulsive shoppers, regularly popping to the supermarket for one item and walking out with 10. Initially we could not work out how we could survive on only $21 for food but once we changed our mindset to seeing it as supplementing what we had already it became considerably easier.

"To succeed at the $21 Challenge you MUST do an inventory, a menu plan and shopping list. Without these three things you are 'winging it' – those three lists are the key to a successful Challenge.

"Since our first Challenge our shopping has gone from being a $300 per week bill to $300 per month! That is a total saving of $12,000 per year."

MANDY DANKO

I am saving $7000 a year!

"The $21 Challenge has changed the way I think about food shopping. I now check my cupboards, fridge and freezer before I shop, and work out what meals I can cook with the food I already have. I then buy only what I need. The $21 Challenge showed me that I could survive for a whole week on so little, and gave me a real sense of achievement.

"Doing the $21 Challenge taught me that I was buying far too much convenience food and paying too much for it. During the Challenge I started shopping around and found great savings.

"Before I discovered Simple Savings, I was an extravagant spender. I loved shopping and was wasteful and thoughtless. My credit cards were maxed out and bills were overdue. I must have racked up hundreds of dollars a year in late payment fees. I bought clothes I never wore, jewelry I didn't even like and as for shoes, I was Imelda Marcos! Now I dislike shopping and find it very easy to stay away from store!

"Since joining Simple Savings I save around $7000 or more a year, have reduced our mortgage and increased our retirement fund dramatically and am a much happier, less stressed, more content wife, mother and woman."

PAT MURPHY

We started our own business!

"With the skills we learned and the money saved doing the $21 Challenge we were able to start our own business! When my husband asked if we could afford for him to take three months off from employed work to work for himself, I was able to confidently say YES – even though it meant a food budget of $50 per week for two adults and two young children – because I'd done it on $21! And we DID. I found it empowering! At the end of the three months we had no meat in the freezer and I discovered quiche in a big way but we became resourceful and we survived – isn't that what all this is about? Realizing that you CAN survive a tight spot? Realizing that it doesn't cost $150 EVERY week to feed your family of four? Realizing that if bananas aren't on special, you can survive a week without them, the way our grandparents did!"

RACHAEL EDWARDS

It can be done!

"I did my week's shopping for $20.60! Wow, how long is it since I shopped for a week with only a basket! I left my wallet behind so I couldn't add one or two extras. I cheated though – I only bought one half a gallon of milk. When I got home, I washed out the old half a gallon bottle, made up a half a gallon of powdered milk, mixed the two lots of milk together in a carton, then halved them between the two cartons. I also realized after I had got home that I was low on vanilla yogurt, but no problem – I just made up a batch of yogurt from scratch. The checkout girl just laughed when I handed over the cash saying 'I did it!'"

KATH CORBEN

"Doing the $21 Challenge was never too hard for me as we are always broke; that's why I joined Simple Savings in the first place! We are a family of six; two adults and four children and last time I did the Challenge it came to $21.60, which included 3 gallons of milk, frozen veggies and some meat. IT CAN BE DONE!"

DEBBIE WARD

Tips for $21 Challenge newbies

The $21 Challenge had its origins on the Simple Savings website as a fun way to motivate members to see how much money they could save in just seven days. We have helped thousands of families get through their week and come out smiling, not to mention better off!

The more basic food staples you currently have to start with, the easier you will find it to get through your first $21 Challenge. The main resources we have are our pantries, fridges, freezers and gardens. We are well aware, however, that in today's busy society, many families live out of bags and cans and do not have the fresh ingredients or freezer stockpile to feed themselves with. No problem – the Challenge is still very doable! You can still make some huge savings even if you don't have a large stockpile to fall back on. The following tips will help make your first Challenge easier.

Make shopping your LAST resort

Many people shop out of habit. They go shopping simply because it's 'shopping day' and stock up on the same old stuff, regardless of whether they actually need to or not. One Simple Savings member discovered when doing her first $21 Challenge that she had no less than 11 cans of corn and nine cans of tomatoes gathering dust in her pantry! She hadn't checked her pantry stocks to see how much she already had; she simply kept on buying without using anything up first.

When you do a $21 Challenge, you make shopping your last resort. You only go when you HAVE to. You only buy what you HAVE to. Your aim is to stay out of the grocery store for as long as you possibly can. Taking a cursory glance around the kitchen before you hit the stores is not enough. You need to take a really good look first and make yourself aware of exactly how much food you have already before you allow yourself to go shopping for more. Give it a try and you will see that doing this alone will save you a lot!

Read the recipes

You don't have to use every recipe in this book, but make sure you at least read through them all. They will show you how to make something out of nothing and offer suggestions for how to use up the various bits and pieces that you do have. They will make you think 'Ooh, we've got this!' or 'I can make that!' Once you see how many ways you can use your available food it will make planning your $21 Challenge meals a lot easier.

Make a menu plan

Making a menu plan is essential for your $21 Challenge as you need to know exactly what you are going to be cooking and exactly what you need to buy. This will keep you out of the stores as much as possible and help you to save as much as possible. If you have never used a menu plan before, now is the time to start! We will show you how in Part 4. Everything you need is right here in this book, or on the Simple Savings website.

Have plenty of snacks

To make your Challenge week as stress-free as possible, it's well worth planning your snacks, as well as main meals. You will be amazed at how many changes you can make to the household during your Challenge without complaint – as long as there are plenty of snacks available. Planning these ahead of time will help you avoid the dreaded 'Mooooom! There's nothing to eat!' You will see from reading the recipes in this book that there are A LOT of quick and delicious snack ideas that can be made from next to nothing.

Pick your timing

We really want you to succeed in saving as much as possible during your Challenge, so we encourage you to pick your timing carefully. For example, don't choose the same week to give up smoking! Tackle one thing at a time. Sometimes it feels as though the entire universe is trying to put the quits on your Challenge – there's an emergency at work, the kids get chickenpox and Aunty Edna announces she's coming to stay. Don't panic! You haven't failed; it's just not the right time for your household. Try again when things have settled down. It's better to start your Challenge off on the right foot than take on too much.

Don't be afraid to ask for help

Whether you are feeding one person or 10, we are with you in your mission to win the Challenge. In fact, help is at hand from all directions! People love it when they are asked for their secret recipes or household tips and are always happy to share them. The library is a great source of help on anything from how to bake a loaf of bread to keeping chickens and of course there is the Internet. Most of all, you can rely on the Simple Savings website and its members to offer advice and support on any questions or difficulties you may be having with the $21 Challenge.

Enter our weekly competition!

As you go through your Challenge, you may well find that you are able to come up with your own tips or fantastic recipes to get you through the week. So that you don't forget them, write down any new things you have learned or successful ways you managed to make a fabulous meal out of nothing. Then send them into us at Simple Savings! We hold a competition every week for the best money saving tip. The winner receives a free 12 month subscription to our paid members area, the Savings Vault!

> To enter the competition go to:
> www.21dollarchallenge.com/competition

Frequently asked questions

Hopefully by now we have gotten you well and truly motivated to make some terrific savings with our $21 Challenge! Before we get into the nitty-gritty, we'll just answer a few frequently asked questions.

Does it HAVE to be $21?

The simple answer is yes – and no! The $21 Challenge was originally intended to feed a family of four; however, the beauty of this Challenge is its flexibility. Thousands of families have successfully adapted the rules to suit larger families. The basic rule of thumb is to add an extra $5.25 into the budget per additional person. It still makes for an incredibly frugal week!

What does my $21 include?

Aha, the golden question! This is an area which is often greatly misunderstood so please read this piece very carefully. The aim of the $21 Challenge is to FEED YOUR FAMILY. You do this using the items already in your fridge, freezer, pantry and garden. Your $21 will simply buy a few extra ingredients to complete your meals.

What about diapers and cleaning products?

Ahem, we'll just repeat the previous answer. Your $21 budget is to FEED YOUR FAMILY! This means you are NOT expected to squeeze baby essentials, cleaning products, gasoline and so on into your $21 budget. You will see how you can easily tailor the Challenge to realistically suit your family's requirements.

Do you expect us to starve?

Absolutely not! The chances of that are very unlikely. You will be amazed how much food you already have in your own kitchen. Okay, it's possible you may need to reduce your portion sizes slightly, eat more veggies and less meat but you never know... your body and the bathroom scales might even thank you!

What are we supposed to eat? Instant noodles?

If you have some in your pantry, then by all means use them up! Contrary to some people's opinions, the $21 Challenge does NOT mean a week confined to toasted sandwiches and instant ramen – although we do have some fantastic toasted sandwich recipes in Part 5! Doing the Challenge will not restrict your diet, in fact quite the opposite. It's far more likely to expand it, because it forces you to find new and creative ways to use up the food in your pantry. This book contains A LOT of examples to help you.

Will it be bad for our health?

A $21 Challenge week is good for you and good for your wallet. For starters, vegetables are cheaper than meat. You will probably eat more of them during a Challenge week to help you stick within your budget so it's even more likely that you will achieve your recommended 5+ daily servings of fresh fruit and veggies. It is also a great opportunity to evaluate everything you have been eating. This could be the start of a healthier you!

Will I have to eat poor quality meat?

Cheap meat does not have to mean yucky meat! That depends largely on two things; your skill as a shopper and your skill as a cook. If you were already a super savvy shopper before you picked up this book then you will no doubt already have a freezer full of delicious, cheap, high quality meat purchased in bulk for about $3 per pound. But if that isn't the case then you either need to eat less meat, learn how to stretch your meat or learn how to cook cheap meat so it becomes tender and delicious. We will show you how to do all these as you read your way through this book.

But, our pantry is bare!

Are you sure the cupboard is truly empty? When most people look in the pantry, they pick up the things in pretty packages first. If they can't see any of their favorite instant food to snack on, they immediately declare that the cupboard is bare. We call it 'Ingredient Blindness'. It's a common illness across most of the developed world, where people's eyes skim over simple plain-colored ingredients such as flour, sugar and rice. They simply don't see them, let alone see them for what they are. These boring looking packages all contain valuable ingredients which will help you make dozens of yummy, filling dishes. They will help you get through your Challenge week and every week thereafter – if only you use them. When you take all these basic food items into consideration, can you honestly say that your cupboard is bare? Fortunately, overcoming Ingredient Blindness is easy. All you have to do is be a little flexible – just like Simple Savings member Kelly van Den Bos!

"I decided this week was going to be a $21 Challenge week in our house. You should have heard my hubby! First he asked when I was going shopping because there was no peanut butter, although we have Vegemite (Australia's favourite spread) and three types of jam. Then he complained there were no apples – I told him there were fresh pears and canned peaches. Next I got told there was 'no cheese', which really meant no sliced cheese as there were two blocks he could slice himself. Finally he tried to tell me there was 'no bread', so I directed him to the 36 burger buns, 36 hot dog buns, six bread rolls and 12 pizza scrolls. But let's not forget, the cupboards are 'empty'!"

How will saving a few hundred dollars this week make any difference to my finances in the long run?

You'd be surprised! The $21 Challenge teaches you to think outside the box and become a more savvy shopper; a skill that will extend well beyond your Challenge week. Look at the big picture – if the tricks you learn from this book result in you saving even an extra $30 on food each week from now on, in 12 months you'll have saved $1560. To show you how easily these small amounts add up, check out the next couple of pages!

Small savings every day on your food bill can add up to huge amounts of money over the course of a year. These numbers show you how quickly

daily saving	monthly saving	yearly saving
$2	$60	$730
$4	$120	$1460
$6	$180	$2190

your savings will add up. The pictures show you all the other things you could be spending that money on instead of wasting it at the supermarket.

daily saving	monthly saving	yearly saving
$8	**$240**	**$2920**
BUS/FERRY TICKET	$240	
$10	**$300**	**$3650**
Mountain Air Cigarettes	Sale $300	
$30	**$900**	**$10950**
COLA		

You CAN make a difference!

See what a difference those few extra dollars can make? You'll be amazed how easy it is NOT to spend money once you really put your mind to it. One of the joys of the $21 Challenge is that you cannot fail. If your usual grocery budget is $200 a week and you manage to get through your $21 Challenge week spending $50, you've still managed to get back $150 on your regular budget. That's a fantastic effort, so be proud!

"Focus on the CHALLENGE rather than the $$. This is a chance to achieve, to improve and to show yourself, and your family, that creatively you can make a difference to your spending, the bills or the credit card balance."

CATHIE ROSS

More than just money

The $21 Challenge began as a novel way to save money, plain and simple. However, it soon became apparent it was far more than just that. The next chapter will open your eyes to many more reasons why we – and thousands of others – all love the $21 Challenge!

Part 2
Top five reasons to take the Challenge

Presumably, the reason you picked up this book in the first place is because you want to save money. The $21 Challenge will certainly help you do that – but if you go into this with the sole aim of saving money you are going to struggle. You have to want more! So your goal for this section is to choose five non-money related reasons to take on the Challenge. To help inspire you to find some, we asked other families to share some of the ways the $21 Challenge has benefited them. Read on and you will see for yourself that the gains are so much more than simply money oriented.

What do you personally want to get out of the $21 Challenge? You may not be sure just yet but as you read through others' experiences, it will become clear. Some may strike a chord and make you think 'That's just what we need!' or 'I want that!' As you go through the stories, circle a rating beneath each of them, with 1 being the least relevant to you and 5 being the most appealing or inspiring. Which ones do you like the sound of most? Which ones would you like to be able to achieve in your own household?

Once you reach the end of the section, write your five favorite reasons for taking the $21 Challenge on the page provided, tear it out and stick it up in a prominent place. By the time you have finished reading the many positives, you should find you are able to fill in your page quite easily!

It will prepare you for financial crisis

Does your household fear an economic crisis? Is being prepared for tough times important to you? The $21 Challenge will equip your entire household with skills to get them through the toughest times — for life.

"The $21 Challenge has been very empowering. After doing it I feel free of money worries, no longer anxious, and more in control of my life. I no longer have to worry about how to afford the next week's groceries and feel less afraid of price rises in the future as I know I could now cope a lot better, having done the $21 Challenge."

ANN KEWLEY

The $21 Challenge will help you prepare for economic crisis.
Is this what you want? Circle from 1 to 5.

1	2	3	4	5
Nope				Absolutely!

It will make you feel good!

It happens to us all from time to time. You feel down in the dumps, even a little bit walked over. The $21 Challenge is just what you need! It will make you feel good about yourself.

"The $21 Challenge is the chance to prove to yourself that you are capable of more than you realize; that if times get tough you can and will manage. It is the personal challenge of a family unit to survive without unnecessary spending – with the 'lifeline' of $21 – for one week – making do with what you have on hand, supporting each other in pooling your resourcefulness, using culinary creativity to provide interesting meals for yourselves. Showing that if for some reason there was a time of no cash for groceries, you could and would survive. It is the chance to learn an important new skill."

DENISE BRUNING

The $21 Challenge will help you feel better about yourself.
Is this what you want? Circle from 1 to 5.

1	2	3	4	5
Nope				Absolutely!

It will give you more control

The $21 Challenge is not just a money saving exercise. It is a control exercise. It's your opportunity to say to retailers 'I'm giving you as little of my money and my life as possible this week. From this moment on I am totally in charge of my kitchen. I am master of my household. I can live on $21 this week!'

"I had to go to the supermarket today to get sour cream for some pumpkin soup – and I resisted so many things that I normally buy. I put back the bottle of Diet Coke and decided having water instead would not kill me! I also put back the milk as I have enough powdered milk to make 5 gallons at home. I put back the crackers for school lunches tomorrow (instead, the kids will finish off the ones that were hiding at the back of the pantry). The bread maker has been working overtime and so far so good – only $4 spent so far. I am in control and keeping it to the absolute minimum!"

KRISTEN MUIR

The $21 Challenge will give you more control in your life!
Is this what you want? Circle from 1 to 5.

1	2	3	4	5
Nope				Absolutely!

It will get you organized

One of the biggest keys to saving money is being organized. When you are organized you are protected from wasting precious time and money. It makes your whole life easier! Unfortunately being organized doesn't come easy to everyone – but the $21 Challenge can help with that. It is a step-by-step, methodical process which has to be followed if you are to succeed. You will have no choice but to be highly organized – so relax and enjoy the feeling!

"Once the Challenge was underway I realized that I had been making really bad decisions when shopping and that I had been careless, as I had never shopped with shopping lists before. I was also embarrassed and annoyed with myself for missing out on savings due to my erratic shopping/spending behavior. The $21 Challenge has changed the way I grocery shop completely. It has forced me to menu plan (which I love!) and eliminated unnecessary and takeout from our diet."

MELINDA HERBERT

The $21 Challenge will help you be more organized!
Is this what you want? Circle from 1 to 5.

1	2	3	4	5
Nope				Absolutely!

It will make you a smarter shopper

The $21 Challenge makes it harder for marketers to persuade you into 'accidentally' buying goods on impulse. When you walk into a supermarket with no real purpose you are easy to manipulate. You are very vulnerable in a place where every single item has its own marketing team all trying to coax your money out of you. But when you do the Challenge you have a goal and a purpose – all of a sudden you become far less easy to suck in. You stop being a shopping victim and start being a Savvy Shopper!

"I learned to look at the bottom and top shelves in the supermarket, no longer just at eye level. That's where all the expensive items are! Since taking the Challenge I now watch everything I spend and write it all down. I am getting rid of debt and saving money for the first time in a long time. The money I saved in my first Challenge paid for a whole year's registration on my car!"

ANNIE PALFREY

The $21 Challenge will make you a smarter shopper!
Is this what you want? Circle from 1 to 5.

1	2	3	4	5
Nope				Absolutely!

It will bring the fun back into cooking

We know how easy it is to get bogged down in the constant drudgery of churning out meals for the family. Instead of resenting your status as cook, revel in it! Take pride in serving up delicious, frugal meals. You are the boss of your kitchen and the $21 Challenge will make it a fun place to be again.

"My family loved trying something 'different' and I was so proud of myself!"

JULIE WILLIS-JONES

"My first Challenge was a great success and I came in just under budget! I felt extremely proud of myself that I could rise to the challenge whilst still serving my family delicious meals that were appreciated by all."

KIM BROOKS

The $21 Challenge will make cooking fun!
Is this what you want? Circle from 1 to 5.

1	2	3	4	5
Nope				Absolutely!

It will make you a domestic goddess!

You don't have to have a voluptuous figure like Nigella Lawson to be a domestic goddess! It's about getting creative with your cooking and having the courage to try something new. Most of the time pretty much anything will work – and if not, you can fix just about any dish with enough pepper or chili or a heaped tablespoon of curry paste! The $21 Challenge will give you the opportunity to experiment.

"I was planning to make shepherd's pie using the leftovers from the leg of lamb the night before but sadly my 16-year-old daughter got to it first! So, I cut off all the remaining meat and found a quarter of a bag of frozen fries, as well as another quarter of a pack of frozen peas, corn and green peppers. I also had a little boiled rice and the leftover gravy I had made for the roast earlier in the week. It all went into a large frypan with some salt and pepper and a little onion powder. It tasted so good all the kids asked for more! I guess my point is that even though some 'throw togethers' don't work out too well, most DO, so give it a go. Give anything a go – you may just be surprised at how well it works out!"

MELISSA SPEK

The $21 Challenge will make you a legend in the kitchen!
Is this what you want? Circle from 1 to 5.

1	2	3	4	5
Nope				Absolutely!

It will show you how to find food when the cupboard is bare

When you do a $21 Challenge you learn how to make your food s-t-r-e-t-c-h further than you ever thought possible. No rushing off to the store when you think the cupboard is bare! You will learn how to find food, even when you think there is none.

"We were on day seven and had no bread, no pita bread, no butter and no meat of any variety! I wanted to have a pity party for one, stamp my feet, throw the kids in the stroller and walk to the store. BUT I foraged in the fridge and found we still had nearly two pounds of grapes; a little soft but the kids happily devoured them for breakfast. I had a coffee and gave myself a stern talking to for being a princess! I had cream and lemonade and jam too, so I made scones for morning coffee and pancakes for lunch. There were even still two nectarines and lettuce, a little cheese and some leftover lasagna. We made it through absolutely fine!"

KRISTY WATSON

The $21 Challenge will teach you how to make your food stretch! Is this what you want? Circle from 1 to 5.

1	2	3	4	5
Nope				Absolutely!

It will cure you of 'Ingredient Blindness'

They may not come in pretty packages but all those boring looking ingredients in your pantry that nobody takes any notice of are worth their weight in gold. They can all be turned into countless super-cheap and delicious meals. Once the $21 Challenge has opened your eyes, you'll never look at them in the same way again!

"It's amazing what you can do with a couple of cans of tuna – tuna pie, tuna casserole, tuna pasta, tuna patties. Also a box of eggs – omelettes, quiche, boiled, fried or scrambled on toast. Some flour, cheese and tomato paste will make you a Margarita pizza on your homemade crust. Two pounds of ground beef will make meatballs, some burgers and a meatloaf or bolognaise sauce. With just a can of tuna, a dozen eggs, some grated cheese and two pounds of ground beef you have the makings of seven or eight main meals."

PAT MURPHY

The $21 Challenge will open your eyes to countless new meals! Is this what you want? Circle from 1 to 5.

1	2	3	4	5
Nope				Absolutely!

It will give you more time

One of our biggest time wasters is having to dash out to the store because we discover we are missing an ingredient or cooking dinner just seems too hard. This won't be a problem during your $21 Challenge – everything you will need for dinner will already be at home!

"I found the process of going through everything and trying to come up with creative ways to use it all to be so refreshing. And the mentality of not being able to go to the store to pick things up means that I actually look forward to the evenings more, because I know that I don't have to go out again once I get home!"

BELLA KNIGHT

The $21 Challenge will give you more time!
Is this what you want? Circle from 1 to 5.

1	2	3	4	5
Nope				Absolutely!

It will help you to be healthier

Clearing out your kitchen for the $21 Challenge is a great way to highlight exactly what your household eats – but be warned, you may not like what you see! If your family is accustomed to eating fast food, the Challenge will help introduce a healthier way of eating. It's not just cheaper; it's better for you. Once you start eating this way, you won't want to go back!

"Yesterday I made the five-cup loaf (so yummy!) to take to a friend's house with some bread. We got home at around 5pm and would have normally been tempted to get fast food... BUT DIDN'T! Instead, I quickly got a salmon quiche and salad ready in no time. Everyone liked it. Even my mother-in-law, who asked for the recipe, after my father-in-law ate it, plus seconds!"

Mia G.

The $21 Challenge will improve your diet!
Is this what you want? Circle from 1 to 5.

1	2	3	4	5
Nope				Absolutely!

It will give you security

The $21 Challenge provides security in the knowledge that you can cope when the unexpected happens. You will no longer have to panic when the dishwasher breaks, something goes wrong with the car or the dog has to go to the vet. You will have all the skills you need to get through and free up some extra money.

"The $21 Challenge has changed my life. I now have peace of mind and don't stress like I used to when I am short on cash. I get paid once a month and before would use my credit card to get me through to the next payday, but NOW I have extra money to reduce the credit card!"

JADE SAWFORD

The $21 Challenge will give you security!
Is this what you want? Circle from 1 to 5.

1	2	3	4	5
Nope				Absolutely!

It will help you get ahead

The $21 Challenge is a wake up call. It gives you the opportunity to get off the never-ending merry-go-round and evaluate your life. The reason so many people work their butts off and never get anywhere is because they're trapped. They are trapped in expensive habits and time sapping routines. They're so busy 'doing', they are never able to find a moment to stop, think about what they are actually doing and how they can improve their situation. The good news is, the $21 Challenge will help you do this so you can stop slipping behind and start getting ahead instead!

"I tried a few $21 Challenges and was coming in at around $40-$50 but this was a huge difference to the $100 plus I was spending, as well as all the through-the-week purchases. My grocery bill has never climbed back to the way it was. I am all set to do a $21 Challenge this week so I can put all the extra money on my electricity bill and get out in front."

JUDY NICKLESS

The $21 Challenge will help you get ahead!
Is this what you want? Circle from 1 to 5.

1	2	3	4	5
Nope				Absolutely!

It will remind you of the joys of cooking from scratch

Over the years, cooking has become a lost art. All you have to do these days to make a meal is open a bag or can. We no longer have the basic survival skills to feed ourselves – but the $21 Challenge will bring them back! People have forgotten that just about anything you find on a supermarket shelf can be made at home. Rediscover the joy of fresh, homemade hot cakes, dripping with butter. Let the divine smell of freshly baked bread waft through your kitchen. When you cook from scratch using real, preservative-free ingredients you will discover not only how much cheaper it is, but how much better it tastes. Your family will love you for it too!

"I have stopped buying pre-made snacks for the children. Instead I make everything from scratch – no more canned pasta sauce. I even make my own pasta now! This week I bought milk, butter, broccoli, carrots and a bag of frozen veggies, apples, onions, garlic, ground beef, peanuts and raisins. We had meat meals four nights of the week and I also made cookies, granola bars and other exciting treats for the children. Total spend for the week was $19."

KELLY HOOPER

The $21 Challenge will remind you how much better food tastes when you make it yourself! Is this what you want? Circle from 1 to 5.

1	2	3	4	5
Nope				Absolutely!

It will help you declutter

During the $21 Challenge you will be using up ingredients you have forgotten about from your pantry, fridge and freezer which, before now, have been lost and hidden among the mess. They stopped being ingredients a long time ago and have just become clutter. Once you start using them up in your Challenge you will suddenly find you have created all this fantastic space. You can find things again! From now on, choosing dinner will be easier because everything is easy to see, you know what you have and can make informed choices.

"My first $21 Challenge went really well. My $21 went on fresh fruit, vegetables and yogurt (we already keep a supply of bread and milk in the freezer). It made me feel really good to be able to clear out the freezer. I did come across a few 'odd' ingredients but nothing that a quick Google search couldn't help me with!"

NATALIE HANCOX-BLACKSHAW

The $21 Challenge will give you more space!
Is this what you want? Circle from 1 to 5.

1	2	3	4	5
Nope				Absolutely!

It will help reduce global warming!

The Western world throws away almost a quarter of all food produced. Each person throws away between 176 lb and 220 lb of food waste every year. Instead of carelessly throwing out pots of leftover this and that, or leaving vegetables to wilt forlornly in the back of the fridge, the $21 Challenge will help you find a way to use them and reduce your household's ecological footprint. Younger family members respond particularly well to the idea of helping the planet – they are the future after all!

"Before, I would never have dreamed of spending time in the garden growing food for us. I had never thought to freeze a vegetable if it wasn't used; I just threw it out. We now have a stockpile of food to fall back on should the need arise. We do not buy fast foods anymore. I have meals I have cooked in bulk and frozen to rely on for those nights I don't feel up to cooking. I have started a vegetable garden and have just bought my first fruit tree!"

MELINDA HERBERT

The $21 Challenge will reduce your household waste!
Is this what you want? Circle from 1 to 5.

1	2	3	4	5
Nope				Absolutely!

It will make your life easier

The $21 Challenge, just like everything at Simple Savings, is here to make your life easier. With the $21 Challenge you learn to live well within your means. If you spend less, you can afford to work less and relax and enjoy life more. It's that simple!

"The $21 Challenge has given us more time together and made us sort out some financial areas of our life that we had been procrastinating on. It's funny, but something as simple as planning our weekly menu has become quite exciting for us and seems to make everything else less of a chore. During the $21 Challenge we noticed that we were relieved of a lot of stress because the week's meals were already planned ahead of time and we knew the ingredients were in the cupboards. My husband and I both enjoy challenges and we are now both challenging each other on the necessity of spending on almost everything!"

ROBYN WALLACE

The $21 Challenge will make your life easier!
Is this what you want? Circle from 1 to 5.

1	2	3	4	5
Nope				Absolutely!

Below is a quick summary of the most popular non-money related benefits gained from doing the $21 Challenge. What do you most want to get out of yours? Read below to refresh your memory, then choose your Top 5 reasons and write them on the next page.

- I want to be prepared in the event of economic crisis
- I want to feel good about myself
- I want to have more control
- I want to be more organized
- I want to be a smarter shopper
- I want cooking to be more enjoyable
- I want to learn how to be resourceful
- I want to be a domestic goddess
- I want to cure my 'Ingredient Blindness'
- I want to have more time
- I want to be healthier
- I want to feel secure
- I want to get ahead
- I want to learn how to cook things from scratch
- I want to declutter my kitchen
- I want to help reduce global warming
- I want to make my life easier!

My top five reasons to take the $21 Challenge

1. _____

   _____

2. _____

   _____

3. _____

   _____

4. _____

   _____

5. _____

   _____

Name: _____ *Date:* _____

Signature: _____

Part 3
How to win the Challenge

So have you chosen your top five reasons for doing the Challenge and written them down? Great! We are going to have fun achieving them.

The $21 Challenge IS fun. It is a game you are going to win! To do this you are going to need a game plan and a strategy. Fortunately we have done this before so we have written out a detailed plan for you to follow.

As the person in charge of your kitchen, you automatically become the team captain for your household's $21 Challenge. It is up to the team captain to take charge, so grab your pen and let's get to work. With the help of this book and us – your own personal cheer squad – you will emerge victorious from the kitchen!

In this all-important section you will:

- learn the rules of the game

- choose your team-mates

- set yourself a saving target

- make a start on your game plan.

Just like any game, the $21 Challenge has rules. It's time to learn yours!

Rules of the $21 Challenge

As previously mentioned, the $21 Challenge is very much a personal challenge, tailored to suit the individual needs of your family. However, there are still a few rules we would like you to adhere to:

Don't cheat!

The aim is to make the most out of what you already have, not go to the supermarket and stock up on everything before the week starts – that's cheating!

Open your eyes

So much of our money is wasted because we suffer from 'Ingredient Blindness'. If we look in the pantry and nothing 'instant' catches our eye, we think there is no food and rush off to the store. Make it your mission during your $21 Challenge week to open your eyes and find creative ways to feed the crew to cure yourself of 'Ingredient Blindness'.

Limit your spending

Living on $21 for a week does not mean you cannot visit the supermarket at all – it just means that when you are there, you cannot spend more than your chosen figure! If you want to cook chicken drumsticks for your family but it's going to take $8 out of your $21 to buy enough drumsticks for a single meal, you might want to come up with something else instead or you're going to find it a real struggle by the time you get to the end of the week! If four carrots are all you are going to need to see you through, then buy only the four you need to stay within your budget, not the whole bag!

Be resourceful

We always keep bread and milk in our freezers so we don't need to buy it during Challenge week, but many people buy a bag of milk powder to see them through once the fresh milk runs out. If you run out of bread, bake your own! Meat is a huge drain on the grocery budget, so if your family are big meat eaters, consider having at least one meat-free dinner during Challenge week. It's a big saver and really good for you too!

What will YOUR Challenge include?

Now you are familiar with the rules, all that remains is to decide who you will be feeding and choose a goal figure for your team to aim for.

Who's on your team?

By this we mean who are you actually going to be feeding in your $21 Challenge week? It's important you work out who your team-mates are before you decide on a savings target. If you want to keep your grocery bill to an absolute minimum, you might want to give this some careful thought.

For example, if you carefully plan your Challenge budget for four people, only to have your daughter's boyfriend with his enormous appetite visit three nights in a row expecting to be fed, then your Challenge is going to be VERY challenging!

So ask your house mates what their plans are for the week beforehand and determine how many people you are going to have to feed. Find out if all the members of your household are coming on board to help you save money with the $21 Challenge. If they are not willing to join in or help you get ahead, they are not your team-mates. Let them fend for themselves for the week. The communal food stocks and your cooking are for team-mates only!

How little can you spend?

How little do you think you can realistically spend on food for the week? Is your Challenge going to cover dinners only, or are you game enough to include everything; dairy, meat, bread, lunches, snacks – the whole shebang? Living on $21 for the week is fairly easy – if you're single. However, if you are a family of five and drinking $40 worth of milk a week it is going to be considerably harder!

IMPORTANT: When setting your target don't do anything that is likely to endanger anyone's health. For example, small children need milk so don't include that in your Challenge budget. If your infants need baby formula don't include that either. The important thing to remember is that what you are really trying to do is see how little you can live off each week, be it $21, $31 or whatever.

How much do you normally spend?

Do you actually know? If not, take the time to write it down. You could be very surprised! Record any money you spend on food during a regular week in a notebook. The first time Jackie did this she was horrified to discover that in a single month, her family had bought food and/or drink no less than 20 days out of 31! That's a LOT of time and money spent shopping!

Writing down and evaluating your spending this way will soon give you an idea of what your family's Challenge goal should be. If after doing so you decide you want to set your spending target at $50 or $100 for the week compared to your usual $200 or $300, that's fine! Any saving is a great saving, so set your first Challenge target within a comfortable reach. Practise makes perfect and you may well find that you are actually able to spend much less when the time comes!

Setting your target!

So what is your target for the week going to be? Are you going for the $21 benchmark? Or are you going with a safer bet for your first go? It's time to make it official!

1. First, we need you to write down everyone you are going to be feeding as your team-mates.

2. Next you need to write down your target figure. How much are you allowing yourself to spend on food this week? $21? $31? $51? What will it be?

3. What will that sum include? Dinners, snacks, lunches, breakfasts? Decide and write it down so everyone will know.

4. Finally, if you reach your target how much will you save? What are you planning to do with that money? Are you saving for a vacation, car registration or building a nest egg? Why is saving this money important to you?

If you are using the book for this exercise, you may want to write in pencil so you can use these pages again. Otherwise feel free to photocopy them or print off as many as you like from **www.21dollarchallenge.com/tools**. If you don't have a computer, ask a friend or family member or use a computer at your local library — they may charge you a small fee to print out the pages.

Fill in the details on your Challenge Target page. Sign it and put it up where everyone will see it to help motivate and remind you.

Our $21 Challenge target

Your name: _____

1. Who are your team mates?

    _____

    _____

2. How little are we going to spend on food this week?

    _____

    _____

3. What will that sum include?

    _____

    _____

4. How much will we save by sticking to that target?

    What are we going to do with our savings?

    _____

    _____

Date: _____   *Signature:* _____

You can download this from www.21dollarchallenge.com/tools

Minor hurdles

We would love to be 100% confident in telling you that everything is going to be perfect on your first Challenge. However, some will embrace the idea with open arms and jump on board the instant they hear about it, others will approach it half heartedly and go along because they respect you, and if you're really unlucky the odd unhelpful so-and-so will do their best to be a right royal pain in the butt during your $21 Challenge. We will politely refer to these people as 'minor hurdles'.

Annoying as they are, we thought it best to give you a little warning, so you can see these hurdles and be ready to jump right over them and keep on running. To make them easy for you to spot, we have plonked them into some common stereotypes and provided you with some examples of the kind of things each are likely to say. These are the underminer, the guilt tripper, the shopping victim, the sponge, the big kid, the snob and the high D.I.

Should you be unfortunate enough to come across any of them in your $21 Challenge week, don't let them get in your way!

The underminer

This person tries to sabotage your $21 Challenge efforts by putting you down. They are lacking in self esteem themselves, so they try to build themselves up by saying hurtful things. They fear that if you succeed you may become too good for them. They may also feel intimidated or jealous of your accomplishments. Why should you save so much money and be so in control of your life when they aren't? Look out for comments such as:

"Here we go – another phase that'll last a day."

"Oh that will be easy – we'll just stock up first!"

"But it's not REALLY $21, is it?"

"It's just a craze. I'll give you 'til tomorrow morning and you'll be buying your cappuccino and muffin like you usually do."

"Yeah right! You stick to a budget? You'll never do it – you've never stuck at anything."

"Huh – you don't have the willpower."

"Count me out – I love my meat and three veggies, and you won't manage THAT on $21 for the week."

"What happens after a week? You'll just go on a spending spree."

Do you recognize this person?

_____

_____

The guilt tripper

This person will use guilt to try to manipulate you into doing things their way. They don't care if it blows your $21 Challenge budget, as long as they get what they want! In many ways they are like the underminer, except instead of belittling you they try to pull at your heart strings. Some typical things they might say include:

"You are so stingy, you never buy us anything good."

"But Mooooom, what about our takeout treat after swimming?"

"If it was something for YOU I bet we could find the money."

"Our mom is so slack. She never gets us any decent food."

"This is all YOUR fault."

"We can't get candy because of the stupid Challenge."

"My friends all get money for the school cafeteria."

Do you recognize this person?

The shopping victim

Shopping victims are easily led and very vulnerable to marketing. They don't *mean* to waste so much money, they just do. They are just as happy to help you spend yours too – even if it is a $21 Challenge week. You can spot shopping victims by their comments:

"This looked so cool. I HAD to buy it!"

"What's the point? You'll only waste the money on something else – you may as well enjoy shopping."

"I saw an ad for it on TV."

"But if you use your credit card it won't count!"

"You need cheering up. We all need to splurge now and again."

"We work hard. We deserve it."

"You might as well spend it. You can't take it with you."

"But it's double reward points at the supermarket this week!"

Do you recognize this person?

_____

_____

The sponge

Sponges are classic freeloaders, they will squeeze every cent they can out of you and think they are clever for doing so. They will eat you out of house and home during your $21 Challenge week! Sponges tend to be very self absorbed – they think only of themselves and don't care if they are a drain on others even when you point it out. They are recognizable by actions more than words.

They arrive just before dinner, eat everything and don't help with the washing up.

They drink all the alcohol and never replace any of it.

They always arrive empty handed, even when you have asked them to bring something.

They just kind of moved in, and you're not quite sure how!

They are always behind with the rent and don't have a problem with it.

They eat all the food and never offer to replace any of it.

They don't care if they use all the hot water.

They always ask you to buy things but don't pay you back.

They don't chip in even though you asked and they have the money.

Do you recognize this person?

The big kid

Big kids are similar to sponges, but there is one very BIG difference. Big kids don't realize they are sponging off you and get very embarrassed if you point it out to them. They have no idea they are strangling your $21 Challenge by scoffing everything in sight. They have been spoiled and take food, electricity and accommodation for granted. You can recognize a big kid by some of the things they say, no matter how old they are!

"Yum! Did you make that for me?" Then proceeds to eat the entire tray of cookies.

"Is there any more food?"

"Oops, were you saving that? I ate it already."

"But I was hungry!"

"You REALLY need to go shopping."

"Er – I don't have enough money. I was hoping you were going to pay for that?"

"You are late! What is for dinner?"

"Why are you looking at me like that?"

Do you recognize this person?

The snob

We all know someone who is just that little bit 'Hyacinth Bucket'. Sorry, but there's no room in a $21 Challenge for snobs! Don't let them blow your budget for the week with their unreasonable demands – they'll survive! Some things you may hear them say include:

> *"You can't seriously expect me to drink **that** wine."*

> *"Eww... I never eat that sort of food."*

> *"I only buy the best."*

> *"I wouldn't be caught dead buying cheap stuff."*

> *"Store brand is for poor people."*

> *"I'm not eating leftovers!"*

> *"You want me to eat that?"*

When you are confronted with such snobbery remind yourself they are mostly victims of marketing. The most expensive item is rarely the best value. **YOU are the smarter shopper!**

Do you recognize this person?

The high D.I.

Socializing with friends and family that have a high disposable income can be really hard during a $21 Challenge. High D.I. friends don't mean to sabotage your budget and most would be horrified if they realized they were putting you in such a tight spot. They have simply forgotten what it's like not to have money to burn. More often than not it's the social situations that destroy the $21 Challenge budget. Some things which might crop up include:

"Oh c'mon, we go out for lunch every Friday – you can't miss it!"

"We're staying at a five star resort. Why don't you come and join us for dinner?"

"Would you like to put $20 towards morning coffee?"

"Forget your boring sandwich. Come and join us at the restaurant for a treat!"

"Sorry for the short notice. Can you pick up a cake from the bakery on the way?"

"We are going to meet at the indoor play gym. There's a restaurant there, so there's plenty of food for the kids."

Do you recognize this person?

Overcoming minor hurdles

'Minor hurdles' have the potential to muck up your carefully planned Challenge budget. If you have already identified someone who may affect your ability to meet your Challenge target, make a note of them, think about some of the possible situations they may present and try to work out a solution to ensure they don't hold you back.

For example, if you know the kids are going to put you on a guilt trip at the supermarket for not buying them candy, try to go shopping on your own. If lunch with friends is on the agenda, offer your house as a venue and bake something basic and yummy. When dealing with a snob during $21 Challenge week, you have to get tough. They can either eat with you, or tell them they can go and eat elsewhere and pay for it with their own money. Don't let their petty wants stop you from getting ahead.

One Simple Savings member dealt with her resident 'sponge' by dishing up dinner only for her family, not the extra, and eating it in front of them too. Apologize and say you don't have enough for them if that makes it easier for you but remember your kitchen is your kitchen, not their own personal restaurant. You get the idea!

> You would be amazed at the ways some clever $21 Challengers have come up with to overcome their minor hurdles!
>
> To read their stories and learn from their successes, check out the Simple Savings Forum in the Vault.

If at first you don't succeed...

Sometimes of course, no matter how well you prepare, those pesky hurdles will catch you unawares and succeed in tripping you up. If this should happen, don't beat yourself up about it. Just get back up, brush yourself off and keep going. You have done your best. There's no need to get angry or upset, just breathe, smile and mentally remind yourself you are going places. Tomorrow is another day. So let's move on to the next section!

"For me, the $21 Challenge has been life changing. It has allowed me to contemplate making a life change to study. I know I can cook well, but when working one gets lazy. Just giving the Challenge a go this week has seen the best meals we have had in ages and I've only spent about $6 so far! I feel empowered and very, very proud of myself putting rusty old skills to work. The first time I attempted the Challenge it was a blowout. I wasn't ready. But now I have a goal in mind it has become a real gift, a reminder of what I can do when I put my mind to it."

MEG MILLEMAGGI

Part 4
The game plan

Your $21 Challenge game plan has three key elements. These elements are essential to helping you succeed and to making your Challenge as easy as possible:

1. Inventory:

First of all you need to figure out what food you already have. This means you are going to have to go through every square inch of your kitchen. We'll help you!

2. Menu plan:

Once you know what food you have, you need to plan what you are going to eat for the week, based around that food.

3. Shopping list:

Your completed menu plan will help you work out how little you will need to buy to get you through the week.

Time for an inventory!

Let's get your game plan underway! Before you can cook anything, before you can buy anything, you need to figure out what food you already have at home right now. You need to reacquaint yourself with your pantry, right to the back of its dark and dusty corners. You need to delve into your freezer and unearth all the food you have forgotten. You need to explore every inch of your fridge, and you need to tally up all the ready-made groceries you have growing in your own backyard courtesy of Mother Nature. You need to do an inventory.

We are going to take you systematically through your home, writing down every item of food that you find as you go. We mentioned this already earlier on, but in case you are only skimming through we are saying it again! Determining how much food you have to start with is vital for your Challenge preparation.

If you are using the book for this exercise, you may want to write in pencil so you can use these pages again. Otherwise feel free to photocopy them or print off as many as you like from:

www.21dollarchallenge.com/tools

If you don't have a computer, ask a friend or family member to print them out for you. You can also use a computer at your local library – they may charge you a small fee to print out the pages.

To succeed at the Challenge, to make it work for you, you need to familiarize yourself with everything you currently have in your cupboards. And we do mean EVERYTHING!

We will tackle this in four sections; pantry, freezer, fridge and garden.

Overhauling your pantry

To begin your inventory, we want you to pull everything out of your pantry and sort it into three piles; regulars, bonus meals and compost.

● **Regulars:** These are the items you use and buy all the time.

● **Bonus meals:** These are goods you bought once-upon-a-time but don't really know what to do with. They have more than likely been sitting on the shelf forever and you could probably make a whole extra meal out of them – if only you could find a way to use them up!

● **Compost:** These are foods which are past their use-by dates and should only be designated to compost or disposed of.

First of all, throw away anything that falls into your 'compost' group – it's definitely time they left the premises for good.

Then write all the items that you use and buy all the time in the 'regular' column of your pantry inventory sheet.

Next write down all the mystery items in the 'bonus meals' column of your pantry inventory sheet. It doesn't matter how small and insignificant the item might be, or if you can't possibly imagine a way to make it into a meal – it is our job to show you how! Just write the item on the list and then place the actual item into a sturdy box or container. From now on, this box of mysterious ingredients will be referred to as your **Bonus Meals Box**. In Part 6 we will show you just how to convert this pile of stuff into marvelous meals.
Your creativity with this box is what the Challenge is all about and could be the difference between a boring week of meals and a gourmet feast!

inventory
exploring your pantry

regulars	bonus meals

You can download this from www.21dollarchallenge.com/tools

Delve into your freezer

As with the pantry clearout, dig deep and pull everything out of your
freezer, writing everything down as you go. Sort your food into the
same three categories as before; regulars, bonus meals and compost.

For example, anything you use and need to replace regularly such
as frozen peas should be written in the 'regular' column on your
freezer inventory sheet. Anything you find that has been sitting
there for an eternity growing icicles because you're not quite sure
what to do with it, such as fava beans, should be added to your
'bonus meals' column. Make sure you put everything back in the
freezer regardless and not in your bonus meals box, unless you like
your food a little soggy…

inventory
delve into your freezer

regulars	bonus meals

You can download this from www.21dollarchallenge.com/tools

Explore your fridge

No doubt you've got the idea now! Declutter the fridge from top to bottom, writing everything down as you go. This time, however, we are going to sort your fridge goods into FOUR groups. Write everything down in the appropriate column on your fridge inventory sheet as you go.

- **Priority:** These are foods which need to be eaten early on in the week or they will go bad, such as a lonely wilted carrot, a bowl of leftovers, bruised fruit and half a chopped onion.

- **Regulars:** These are foods you eat all the time, such as milk, margarine and in our households, ketchup!

- **Bonus meals:** These are things which have either snuck to the back of the fridge and are hiding in corners or cluttering up the door of your fridge. Things like the three-quarters full jar of corn relish and the last lump of Havarti cheese all have the potential to be turned into a meal, so write them in this column.

- **Science experiments:** We all have these lurking in the fridge! These are the foods which make you want to get out the rubber gloves and a plastic bag, take a deep breath and put a plug on your nose before you approach them. Even though it is tempting to leave any science experiments in the fridge for another day or two in the hope someone else will clean them up… even if you are waiting to discover if the milk in the container will turn into cheese if you leave it long enough… when we say, 'clean out the fridge', we mean the ENTIRE fridge. Once you have safely removed them, we'll leave it up to you how you choose to dispose of them!

Once you have sorted all the items in your fridge, write down the high priority foods, the regulars and the bonus meals items onto your inventory sheet so you can refer to it later to plan your meals.

inventory

decluttering the fridge

priority	bonus meals
regulars	

Garden groceries

If you are lucky enough to have some vegetables or herbs already growing at home, don't forget to go out and check these too. You have three categories to sort these into:

- **Priority:** These are plants which need to be eaten or cooked within a day or two in order to avoid them going to waste.

- **Bonus meals:** These are things which you planted to see how they would go but aren't quite sure what to do with them. Fiona has done this with radishes. Once they were ready she just sort of left them in the ground and stared at them for several weeks wondering what to do with them all! Jackie once grew a wonderful crop of pak choy, even though she had no idea what she was supposed to use it for! Don't forget to search around for food plants you have forgotten about such as mint or oregano. Mint grows wild all over the place so it's very likely you have some without even realizing!

- **Ready this week:** This one is self-explanatory; simply write down any food you think will be ripe for picking and eating this week so you can be sure to use it up. If you have chickens, write down how many eggs you expect to get this week. If you are lucky enough to have poultry or 'homegrown' meat ready for slaughter, add this in too. Jackie's family often go fishing when the cupboards are bare. If you regularly catch fish, put your estimated catch here too. Make sure you write EVERYTHING on your list so you won't forget anything when the time comes to write your menu plan.

inventory
garden groceries

priority	bonus meals
ready this week	

Now you have made your inventory you are going to feel much more in control. Are you surprised to discover just how much food you actually have? Isn't it great to know exactly what food you have in your house right now! From now on, every time you use something from your inventory, cross it off. You will be able to see at a glance what you have and how much headway you are making. You will also discover how much easier it is to simply eat what you already have at home, rather than traipse off to the store. Give yourself a pat on the back every time you use something up!

You have earned yourself a breather so make yourself a cup of tea. Sit down with your inventory sheets and review your list of food and ingredients. Think about how you can use them up in your $21 Challenge. 'Would that make a good sandwich topping?' 'Could these go in a soup, casserole or pie?' 'What can I do with those things?' There could be a lot to take in but don't worry if you find that you draw a complete blank. Even if you come across an item you have absolutely no idea what to do with, don't panic! We are here to help you.

It's time to buckle down to the main part of your game plan – your menu plan!

How to menu plan

Menu planning can transform your kitchen into a blissfully organized place where all kinds of delicious aromas waft about and mouth-watering meals miraculously appear with minimum stress and fuss. Even better, they arrive on the table with little or no impact on your bank balance. Once you give menu planning a try you won't believe how much you will consistently be able to save on your food bill and your family will eat a healthier, more varied diet than ever before. All it takes is a piece of paper stuck to your fridge!

Writing a menu plan for the first time can be daunting, however, so we thought it would be helpful to show how we use the food we unearth in our inventory to come up with ideas for meals.

As a rule when menu planning, you decide what you want to eat during a particular week first and then buy those ingredients accordingly – but not during a $21 Challenge! With this menu plan you have to work backwards. The point is not to base your plan around what you need to buy, but what you already HAVE. Before you can buy anything else, you need to see if you can turn all the things you have just found cluttering up your cupboard into actual meals. Then, and only then can you determine exactly what you are going to NEED to buy during your Challenge.

The first $21 Challenge menu plan

The best way to explain how the $21 Challenge Menu Plan works is to share Barbara's original menu plan from the first ever $21 Challenge. Her main focus was to make her $21 stretch to cover the family's evening meals together. While she didn't write down her plans for lunch or breakfast rest assured they did eat them! We will show how to include lunch and breakfast in your menu plan later on in this section.

Here's how Barb got started with her $21 Challenge. Before spending her $21 she did a quick inventory and found she had a can of tuna, two chicken breasts, two frozen fish fillets, apples, pumpkin, potatoes, lemons, a box of cereal, milk and bread already at home. Here is how she made it last the week:

Monday Barb used frozen fish fillets for dinner and bought sausages for her teenage boys. She disguised the pumpkin by mixing it with some potato and found a bag of dried peas left over from a school camp.

Tuesday she bought some broccoli and a one pound combo pack of ground beef and sausage meat and made meatloaf. She baked potatoes from her cupboard.

Wednesday she used one chicken breast and lemons to make lemon chicken and saved one breast for Friday.

Thursday   she used the can of tuna to make tuna patties and bought half a cabbage to make coleslaw (she only used half the cabbage). One boy wouldn't eat the tuna so there went Barb's spare chicken!

Friday   she bought some pasta and used leftover salami and canned tomatoes to make a sauce to go with it.

Saturday   she used the rest of the cabbage and some more of the ground beef to make a chow mein. She saved a small portion of ground beef for Sunday.

Sunday   she purchased some pie crust and used the last of the ground beef to make a family sized pot pie.

As you can see it's really a case of looking at what you have and planning ahead. All Barb ended up buying was her ground beef and sausages, broccoli, cabbage, pasta and pie crust – pretty small shopping list for a whole week – and nobody complained about going hungry!

So you see how it works? Barb originally shared her $21 Challenge menu plan with Jackie. After learning how Barb did it, Jackie couldn't resist giving the $21 Challenge a go too! Here is Jackie's first $21 Challenge menu plan, based on her inventory. From her pantry, fridge, freezer and garden inventories she was able to come up with the following meals to use up some of the things she found. Most of the recipes she used can also be found in this book!

Jackie's first menu plan

Monday **Creamy chicken curry with rice**. The easiest curry recipe ever and one of hubby, Noel's favorites! Found a can of creamy chicken soup in pantry left over from when my youngest had his tonsils out. Already have sour cream in fridge, chicken pieces in freezer and rice in pantry.

Tuesday **Salmon quiche with green vegetables**. Found a 15½ oz can of pink salmon in pantry. Will need to buy eggs but have cheese on hand, chives and broccoli in the garden and plenty of other veggies in the freezer.

Wednesday **Creamy pasta**. My favorite recipe for using up evaporated milk! Found a can of lite evaporated milk in the pantry. Also have pasta in pantry and mushrooms, green peppers and cheese in the fridge, will just need to buy a couple of zucchini or can substitute for something else if zucchini too expensive. Will grab a piece of steak from the freezer for Noel to go with it.

Thursday **Star Wars hotpot**. Haven't made this for years! Perfect for the crockpot too, just throw it all in and forget about it. I remembered this recipe when I found a couple of cans of tomatoes and a can of sweet corn in the pantry. You also need sausages and bacon, which I already have in the freezer, onions which I have and potatoes, which I'm going to have to buy.

Friday   **Homemade burgers**. I found enough ground beef when doing my freezer inventory to make a family favorite, homemade burgers. I already have all the other ingredients I need in the pantry, just need to buy some burger buns. Will use some of the bought potatoes to make homemade potato wedges too.

Saturday   **Slow cooked French onion chicken**. I found this recipe on the Simple Savings website – it's a great way to use up the package of onion soup from the pantry! Another good crockpot recipe too. Will have enough chicken pieces left in the freezer from Monday and can also use up the other can of tomatoes from the pantry. Nice with rice or mashed potatoes, both of which I will have, along with more vegetables from the freezer. I always prepare and freeze my fresh vegetables as soon as I buy them. It's a big time, money and space saver and means we can always enjoy a large variety of vegetables all year round.

Sunday   **Roast dinner**. We always have a Sunday roast, just as my mom raised me! Have plenty of pork in the freezer so will roast one of those. Will still have plenty of potatoes to roast, along with all necessary ingredients for Yorkshire pudding and of course all the veggies I need in the freezer.

That's about it I think! We never eat dessert as we're always too full. I have bananas in the freezer to make banana muffins for lunchboxes and after school snacks and oats in the pantry to make ANZAC biscuits (page 185) . So my shopping list for the week looks like this:

Potatoes

Milk

Eggs

Bread

Burger buns

Zucchini (if not too expensive)

Tomatoes for sandwiches ($2 for a huge bag from a local lady selling them outside her house)

Potato chips for the boys' lunchboxes

Grand total: $17

After seeing how easy it was to live on such a small amount, Jackie couldn't wait to share Barb's story with other Simple Savings members. From the moment they heard it, people 'got' the concept and went rummaging through their kitchens to see how little they too could get away with spending. They started getting creative and diversifying where necessary in order to stay away from the stores. Before we knew it, everyone was menu planning!

We learned that to make menu planning work for us, it was important to find a planner that suited our family's needs. So we came up with our own! We'll take you through our individual methods here. Both are very different – see which one suits your household best!

Jackie's three-step guide

Jackie's way of menu planning is simple. Just three steps and you're done! Here they are:

Step 1. Choose your recipes

To choose your recipes simply consult your recipe books, go online, whatever your preferred method is. When you find a recipe that matches what you have on hand, pick a day on your planner and write it down. I find that just going through my recipe book automatically gives me a balanced menu for the week, by the time I have chosen meals from the meat, poultry, fish and vegetable sections. I write the book title and page number next to the recipe for each day; it makes them easier to find when the time comes to cook. As the family only eats together for our evening meal, I don't worry about planning breakfast or lunch but you'll see there is an extra column under the last day for baking – that's to remind me to actually do some. It really works! I choose one cookie recipe and one cake or muffin recipe to make per week and this gives us enough for the week's lunches and afternoon snacks. This alone saves me a small fortune on lunchbox fillers and means the family always has plenty to eat during $21 Challenge weeks.

Step 2. Make your shopping list

While you're filling in your planner, take note of the recipe ingredients and write down any that you do not already have. By the time you have finished, you have your ready-made shopping list for the week. I'm then able to take care of any necessary food shopping in one visit – no need to set foot in a supermarket for the rest of the week because I know I have everything I need for our meals. Too easy!

Step 3. Put it up!

All you have to do now is put your menu planner in a prominent place and remember to check it each day. My planner is on my fridge. I look at it each morning and go right to the freezer to take out any meat that needs defrosting. I know exactly what I am doing for dinner and how long it will take. It really is that easy!

We eat consistently on time because I'm not flapping around trying to think what to cook and throwing any old thing together. I'm enjoying cooking new things and the family is enjoying eating them. Because the meals are balanced, it's much easier to adapt them to suit everyone's preferences and we are all eating far more healthily. I know exactly what food I need from week to week, I don't need to make any mercy dashes to the local store and it has also helped me to organize my pantry long-term. It's proven such a big saver that I plan my menu every week, not just for $21 Challenges!

menu planner

day of week	name of recipe	book and page no.
monday		
tuesday		
wednesday		
thursday		
friday		
saturday		
sunday		
baking		

You can download this from www.21dollarchallenge.com/tools

Fiona's life planner

Fiona always thought menu planning was a lovely idea in theory but it never seemed to work for her – until someone gave her a family organizer. Once Fiona started writing down the family's activities for the week she realized that the organizer was the perfect tool to help plan her meals too. She didn't just need a menu planner, she needed a life planner. At last she had come up with a personalized system that works!

This planner doesn't just save Fiona money – it also saves time and makes her life much easier. Before we explain how it works, go to Fiona's completed planner on page 100. Read through it and you will see a row for each stage: **Activities, Food and Prepare**. You will also see columns for each meal throughout the day, including snacks, which correspond to the time of day you are likely to eat the meal. There are also codes such as (GA) and (L). Don't be confused – Fiona will explain it all as we go! Let's start with the activities.

Activities

Filling in your activities is pretty easy. Simply write down the activities your household has planned for the week, next to the meals they are closest to. School, swimming, sports events, meetings, days you will be late home from work – anything you will need to prepare food for, or which may affect your ability to prepare food.

Food

Once you have filled in your activities, you can look at your planner and instantly see which days are going to be busy or quiet. (You'll see I write this in too.) This makes planning your meals for the week so much easier. I simply choose appropriate recipes for each day, such as quick and easy 'no-brainer' meals on busy days and more time consuming dishes on quieter days.

Remember, to succeed at a $21 Challenge week you need to buy as little food as possible. I start by doing an inventory (as covered in full at the start of this section) and take note of all the food I have to work with. I try to choose nutritious food from the start, but I always go through my planner at the end to make sure the family are getting their five plus servings of fruit and vegetables each day.

Sneaky tricks!

I also have three sneaky tricks which I include in my planner to help make my Challenge week a breeze! The first is to cook in bulk, to make what I call 'get ahead' meals. The second is to rummage through my pantry for any forgotten ingredients which I can use to make an extra or bonus meal. The third is to plan for leftovers. I highly recommend trying each of these tricks at least once during your Challenge week to save yourself time and help you get into the swing of things. Here's how they work:

(GA) = Get Ahead

'Get ahead' meals are the ultimate cheat, and I try to squeeze in as many as possible. This is when you cook double or triple batches of food; eat one batch that day and pop the rest in the freezer so you won't have to cook later. They can be simple shortcuts such as making a week's worth of sandwiches in one go so you only have to pull them out of the freezer each morning. You can save yourself from having to cook dinner one night by making a triple batch of bolognaise. Or, you can make a big batch of cookies. Yummo!

(BM) = Bonus Meals

During a $21 Challenge week you will have great fun being creative and searching around your pantry for long lost goodies. However, turning clutter into cuisine often requires thought. So try to schedule your bonus meals for quieter days, when you can experiment with ingredients without the pressure of having to get the kids to football practise.

(L) = Leftovers

Stretching your food as far as you can will make your week easier. See how many different ways you can turn last night's dinner into something completely new, e.g. leftover roast meat into a stir-fry or pie, or pumpkin soup into pumpkin scones.

Preparation

Once you have worked out all the meals you are going to have during your Challenge week, see if there are other ways you can make your life easier by preparing some of the food beforehand. During my failed menu planning, there were four things I always forgot to do: I would forget to prepare certain foods beforehand. I would forget to defrost food, so it wasn't ready to be cooked when I wanted to cook it. I would forget to soak or marinate things, so it was always too late to cook the dish by the time I remembered it. Finally, I would forget to freeze things ahead of time, so when I went to the freezer to get something out, it wasn't there! Very frustrating! So I added a 'preparation' row in my life planner, which is invaluable in stopping me from making these mistakes.

Run through everything you are planning on eating and see if anything needs to be cooked ahead of time, defrosted, soaked or frozen. If it does, write it down in your 'preparation' row – as you will see below, I use simple codes on my planner.

(C) = Cook ahead

(D) = Defrost

(S) = Soak

(F) = Freeze

Nutrition

When you have done all these things, make sure you do a final fruit and vegetable count at the end. Will everyone be getting their essential five plus daily servings of fruit and veggies? Once you are happy with your choices, write your shopping list for the week.

My shopping list

Time for the real test! Here is where I find out if my menu plan comes in under the $21 target or if I have to change some meals to win the Challenge. I find the easiest way to work out my shopping list is to look at each day on my menu planner and work out a) all the food I will need to get through that day, and b) where that food is going to come from.

Monday: Will need bag of apples ($3) and oranges ($3). Bread and milk in freezer. Lots of rice crackers, pumpkin, tuna, sushi rice, vinegar, sugar, seaweed, flour in cupboard. Eggs and celery leaf from garden.

Tuesday: Will need broccoli ($2). Carrot in fridge. Nuts in cupboard. Eggs and herbs from garden. Milk in freezer.

Wednesday: Will need more carrots ($3), beans ($1) and celery ($2). Herbs, eggs, spinach from garden. Plenty of flour, brown sugar, vanilla extract and oatmeal in cupboard. Margarine in fridge. Milk and banana for ice cream from freezer.

Thursday: Will need lettuce ($2), cucumber ($2). Nuts, potato, cordial syrup and chickpeas in the cupboard. Milk and sausages in freezer. Pear in bottom of fridge.

Friday: Buy nothing. Milk, bananas, sandwiches, chicken and bread in freezer. Lemons, eggs from garden. Oil, herbs, peanut butter, sugar, vanilla extract and garlic in cupboard. Veggies in fridge from Wednesday.

Saturday: Buy nothing. Milk and bananas from freezer. Canned fruit, gelatin, cordial syrup, flour, crackers in cupboard. Eggs from garden. Salad ingredients saved from Thursday.

Sunday: Buy nothing. Kids will have to cook with ingredients on hand, probably chocolate cake. Cocoa, sugar, flour in cupboard. Margarine in fridge. Bolognaise from freezer. Eggs from garden.

According to my list, all the items we will need for the week are:

Apples	$3
Oranges	$3
Broccoli	$2
Carrots	$3
Beans	$1
Celery	$2
Lettuce	$2
Cucumber	$2
Estimated spend for week:	**$18**

Fiona's life planner

CODES: Get ahead (GA) Leftover (L) Cook early (C) Soak (S) Defrost (D) Freeze (F)

		breakfast	snack
monday	activity:	Yoga	Work, school, day care
	food:	Muffins, flat bread	Apple, custard
	prepare:	(GA) Make double sandwiches & freeze for Fri	(L) Make enough pumpkin soup for dinner & scones
tuesday	activity:		School
	food:	Muffins, flat bread	Apple
	prepare:	Make sushi rolls	
wednesday	activity:	**BUSY**	School
	food:	Muffins, oatmeal	Apple
	prepare:	Make sushi rolls	(GA) Cook triple bolognaise & cookies - for Sat & spare
thursday	activity:	**QUIET**	Work, school, day care
	food:	Muffins, oatmeal	Apple
	prepare:	Make sushi rolls	
friday	activity:	Kids cooking	Work, school, day care
	food:	Fabulous fruit smoothie	Apple
	prepare:	(GA) Grab sandwiches from freezer	(GA) Make big batch of hummus
saturday	activity:	Kids cooking	Shopping
	food:	Fabulous fruit smoothie	(GA) Carrot, crackers and hummus, cordial syrup
	prepare:	Fruit Jell-O, flat bread	
sunday	activity:	**LAZY**, kids cooking	Kids cooking
	food:	Kids' choice, flat bread	Kids' choice
	prepare:		

lunch	snack	dinner
School, shopping		
Sandwiches	Fruit and crackers	(L) Reheat pumpkin soup
		(C) Make sushi rice, (F) popsicles for lunches, (D) milk
School		
Tuna sushi rolls	Pumpkin scones, fruit	Veggie stir-fry, fruit
		(D) Take out ground beef, (F) popsicles for lunches, (D) milk
School	Swimming	
Tuna sushi rolls	Cookies	(GA) Bolognaise, banana ice cream
		(C) Make sushi rice, (F) freeze popsicles, (D) take out sausages and milk
School		Kids are cooking dinner
Tuna sushi rolls	Oranges, nuts and cordial syrup	Sausages, salad, noodles. Baked fruit
		(S) Soak chickpeas for hummus, (D) take out chicken
School		
Monday sandwiches	Crackers and hummus	Peanut butter and chicken stir-fry with veggies and noodles
		(F) Freeze drinks for Saturday
Shopping	Park	
Flat bread, water	Cookies, water	Baked potato, veggies, chicken. Fruit Jell-O
	Beach	
(GA) Crackers, carrots and hummus	Cookies, fruit, water	Bolognaise from freezer, custard
		(GA) Make big batch of custard for school lunches

weekly life planner

This planner has been designed to photocopy neatly on to two pages. Simply align the chart area on the photocopier. You may also download the weekly life planner from **www.21dollarchallenge.com/tools**

		breakfast	snack
monday	activity:		
	food:		
	prepare:		
tuesday	activity:		
	food:		
	prepare:		
wednesday	activity:		
	food:		
	prepare:		
thursday	activity:		
	food:		
	prepare:		
friday	activity:		
	food:		
	prepare:		
saturday	activity:		
	food:		
	prepare:		
sunday	activity:		
	food:		
	prepare:		

lunch	snack	dinner

Our life planner has made life easier in ways I would never have imagined. The kids absolutely love it. In the old days they would get home from school, ask what there is to eat and expect me to prepare food for them. Now they go to the planner, read it and get the food themselves. IT IS SO EASY! The whining, moaning and complaining (mostly done in frustration by me) has gone. Life is better. I love my planner!

Hopefully this section has really gotten your brain ticking about some of the things you can do to get through your own $21 Challenge. We've shown you how we go about planning our Challenge weeks, now it's your turn. Try filling out your menu planner! With the help of your inventory, you should find that coming up with a week's worth of meals is a lot easier than you thought! As you progress, you may even find that you are able to come up with your very own way to menu plan. If you do, take the time to share it with us at Simple Savings! You could help someone else succeed at their $21 Challenge – and you could win yourself a Vault membership at the same time!

Once you have filled out your menu plan, you're ready for the next step. It's a simple step but an extremely important one. You've already seen how we use our menu plans to create shopping lists for the week and make sure we come in under budget. Now it's time for you to do the same.

Your $21 Challenge shopping list

One of the first and most basic tips for savvy shoppers is 'shop with a list and stick to it'. Making this list is essential for your Challenge. You have to make a detailed shopping list before you spend a single cent or even set foot in a store if you are to reach your target and make it through the week having spent as little as possible. Go through your menu plan recipes and write down any items you are going to have to buy. It will soon become clear whether you are going to be able to stay within your budget. If not, you may need to rethink some of those recipes!

Once you have filled out your shopping list you are ready for the final stage of your $21 Challenge preparation – the checklist!

Don't forget to use a pencil if you want to use these pages again in future. You can of course download more copies any time from: **www.21dollarchallenge.com/tools**

Shopping list

Here is your official $21 Challenge shopping list! It's essential that you fill it in so you know for sure how close you are to target. How little will your groceries cost this week? Be sure to include any non-food items you need in the space at the bottom too, just don't include those in your Challenge budget. This should be the smallest shopping list you have ever written!

shopping list

days	ingredients needed	cost
monday		
tuesday		
wednesday		
thursday		
friday		
saturday		
sunday		
	week total	
non-food items		

You can download this from www.21dollarchallenge.com/tools

Challenge checklist

Are you ready to do the Challenge?

Have you:

Chosen five reasons to do the Challenge? ☐

Read the rules? ☐

Chosen your team-mates? ☐

Set your targets? ☐

Identified and planned for minor hurdles? ☐

Overhauled your pantry? ☐

Delved into your freezer? ☐

Explored your fridge? ☐

Looked for groceries in your garden? ☐

Chosen a style of menu planning? ☐

Read through the recipes? ☐

Gone searching for bonus meals? ☐

Worked out what meals you can make? ☐

Written them on your menu plan? ☐

Made sure you have included plenty of fruit and veggies? ☐

Made sure you have plenty of snacks? ☐

Written a shopping list? ☐

When you can check all of the above, you are ready, so GO FOR IT!

You can do it!

Congratulations! You have completed all the necessary steps and can consider yourself well prepared. We wish you and your team all the best for a successful Challenge week. We know you can do it!

As you go through your Challenge, you will find that the steps you have taken to prepare for your $21 Challenge have uncluttered your brain, as well as your pantry! From now on it will be much harder for grocery stores to persuade you to part with your money.

Every supermarket's goal is to entice you to spend more in their store. Most people are usually too busy trying to remember what they need to buy and wander around aimlessly. They end up picking up all sorts of other things along the way and spend way more than they planned. But not you – not anymore!

When you go into the store this week, you can be 100% confident of sticking to your list because you know exactly what you have to get and will not be distracted by tempting displays or flashy marketing. You are organized. You are in control. You are well on your way to becoming a smarter shopper!

Part 5
Great recipes

The following collection of recipes have all been tried, tested and recommended by Simple Savings staff, members and other families who have used them with great success in their $21 Challenges. They have been included because, unlike most recipe books, they are based around everyday ingredients, that according to our members, most households usually have on hand. This should make it much easier for you to match up the items you find in your fridge, freezer, pantry and garden inventories and find a way to use them up in your menu plan. Another bonus of using these recipes is that (again, unlike most recipe books), you shouldn't have to go out and buy half a dozen ingredients before you can make them!

As is the case with many 'tried and true' favorites, the majority of recipes in this book have been passed down through generations or word of mouth, hastily scribbled down on scraps of paper, or shared on the Simple Savings website. Wherever possible we have endeavored to trace the original source of the recipe and give credit where it is due. Should you discover we have missed one inadvertently, we apologize sincerely!

The main focus of the $21 Challenge is on dinner, simply because it is the one meal where the whole family gets together to eat the same thing. Breakfasts, lunches and snacks vary greatly and are usually an individual choice; however, we have included some suggestions for tasty breakfasts, lunches and snacks to inspire you and fill rumbling tummies on days when you're running low on ideas or ingredients!

Brilliant breakfasts

'Surprise' cereal

We all have them – boxes of cereal with 'odds and ends' in them. New brands that the kids didn't like, muesli dregs, Rice Krispie remnants and so on. Use them up by mixing them all together to make a brand new 'surprise' cereal. This is also a great way of reducing your cereal costs long term, as it enables you to mix a cheap, generic cereal with a more expensive one. Your family gets the same taste but it only costs you half as much!

Go to work on an egg!

Egg on toast makes a filling and nutritious breakfast and it's actually much cheaper than cereal. Enjoy your eggs boiled, poached, scrambled or fried with toast. To make it taste extra special put a little bit of your favorite spread such as pesto, cheese or mustard on your toast before eating it with your egg. Jackie has been doing this for ages after hearing about it years ago from Billy Connolly on TV. You have to try it!

Brown rice for breakfast

Other countries enjoy rice and noodles every day for breakfast – so can you! For a tasty, filling, super healthy, low-fat, low-GI and low-cost breakfast, try brown rice! It may sound bland and boring but you can flavor it differently each morning and enjoy it hot or cold. Cook in bulk and simply freeze in portion sizes. At breakfast time, you can simply remove one from the freezer and 'zap' it in the microwave before flavoring it.

Outstanding oatmeal

Oatmeal is the tastiest, healthiest and best value cereal on the market. If the one thing that you take out of this Challenge and continue to do is switching to oatmeal every morning, then your Challenge is a success!

Prepare your oats following the instructions on the box and then turn them into something special with these scrumdiddlyumptious recipes. While you are there can you say, supercalifragilisticexpialidocious oatmeal? Serves 4.

Yummy and decadent

Anyone with a sweet tooth is going to love these variations. It's like starting the day with an energy packed dessert!

Banana butterscotch: Mash together 2 tbsp brown sugar, a banana and 2 tbsp butter. Stir through your hot oatmeal. Serve with a sprinkling of cinnamon, nutmeg or ginger.

Berry burst: Put a cup of fresh or frozen berries, 2 tbsp powdered sugar, a dash of lemon juice and ¼ tsp vanilla extract in a saucepan and stir on a medium heat until bubbling hot. Take off the stove and whisk vigourously. Stir through your hot oatmeal.

Speedy varieties: If you would like to dress up your regular oatmeal in a hurry, try putting one of these on top and then stir them through.

- a squeeze of lemon, 1 tbsp of granulated sugar and a sprinkling of ground ginger
- a dash of Nesquik or drinking chocolate and sugar
- 1 tbsp of both peanut butter and jelly
- a squirt of maple syrup, honey, chocolate or toffee sauce.

Tahitian oatmeal: This tasty, tropical way to start your day is a little different from the recipes above. When preparing your oatmeal, swap your milk or water for one can of coconut milk or cream, 2 tbsp shredded or dessicated coconut, ¼ tsp of ground cardamon, a pinch of powdered cloves and sugar to taste. Whilst cooking, top up the fluid level with water or milk. Serve topped with extra coconut and canned pineapple (or passionfruit, banana or mango) - yummy!

Healthier alternatives

These variations include less sugar but a whole lot of taste!

Supercalifragilisticexpialidocious oatmeal: This ultimate 'to-go' breakfast, needed the ultimate word to describe it. You can mix it up beforehand, put into containers in the fridge for up to three days and then take one in the morning to eat at work. In a bowl, mix 1½ cups of rolled oats, ½ cup apple or pear juice along with 1 grated apple, ½ cup almond slivers (or other nuts), yogurt and milk to cover. Stir and then dish into four smaller containers. Store in the fridge. Great eaten hot or cold!

Healthier than healthy: A scrumptious, energy packed breakfast if you're watching your waistline. Cut up 12 dried dates, stir through your dried oats and then cook as normal for a naturally sweetened delight. Top with a sliced banana or strawberries and crushed nuts.

Dried fruit salad: We all have packages of dried fruit lurking in the recesses of our pantry. Bring them out into the light and super charge your energy levels! Top your cooked oatmeal with a flavorsome assortment of cranberries, apricots, golden raisins, raisins and currants, a spoonful of honey plus a sprinkling of almond slivers, sunflower seeds, pumpkin seeds or other nuts.

Sophie's homemade yogurt

Most people think that when they run out of yogurt they have to go to the store to buy more, but it is not true. You can make it yourself and you don't even need a yogurt maker. We have got one of our favorite frugal chefs, Sophie Gray from Destitute Gourmet, to show you how.

This recipe makes 2.5 cups of yogurt for a fraction of store prices and it's so much more rewarding to make your own too. It just takes a little time as you need to 'incubate' the yogurt for 8 to 10 hours in a warm place. A yogurt maker will incubate the milk culture at exactly the right temperature so use one if you have it. If not, try either a warmed Thermos or glass preserving jar. Set it in a cooler full of hot water or wrap in a blanket and place in the hot water cupboard.

2.5 cups milk (use whole or skim milk, or milk made from powder)

*1 tbsp fresh, natural yogurt containing live cultures
(this is your 'starter')*

¼ cup milk powder for a thicker, creamy consistency (optional)

Heat the milk to a simmer, then cool till lukewarm.

Add the yogurt starter (your tablespoon of fresh yogurt) and mix it in well. Pour the liquid into a warmed jar or Thermos and seal.

Leave undisturbed in a warm place for 8-10 hours. The yogurt is ready when it is set. Pour off any watery liquid and store in the fridge till required. Before you flavor the yogurt, scoop out one tablespoon of yogurt to use as the starter for your next batch.

Tips and tricks

- Homemade yogurt may be sweetened with sugar, honey or molasses. Add fresh or pureed fruits or use in sauces and baking.

- If your yogurt is too thin add more milk powder.

- If there is a lot of watery whey in the container the yogurt may have simply incubated too long.

- The culture weakens over time. You will need to use a new starter every fifth batch or so.

- Insulated yogurt canisters can be picked up second-hand very cheaply.

RECIPE COURTESY OF SOPHIE GRAY, DESTITUTEGOURMET.COM

Fabulous fruit smoothies

Fruit smoothies are a favorite breakfast in our house. They are quick to make and even quicker to eat. All you need is some milk, protein, fruit, ice and flavoring then whiz it in the blender. We have our own chickens so for protein we add fresh safe raw eggs. If you don't have a safe raw egg supply, then you can add whey powder or a nut meal for protein.

Our favorite smoothie is banana. When the store has too many overripe bananas and are selling them at a discount, we buy up big. Slice them up and freeze them in containers. Then use them to make this delicious shake whenever you like. The whole family will love them!

Pancakes

Have you ever made pancakes from scratch? Every weekend Shelley, who you will meet on page 148, makes them for her very lucky family from the basic ingredients of flour, sugar, milk and egg. This recipe makes 4 delicious pancakes.

1 cup flour

2 tsp baking powder

2 tbsp sugar

½ cup oats (optional)

Pinch of salt (optional)

1 cup milk (with a dash of vinegar to sour it)

1 egg

Butter to grease the pan

Sift flour and baking powder together into a large bowl. Add the other dry ingredients. Make a well in the center and add the egg. Slowly pour in your milk, stirring constantly with a spoon, until you have made a smooth but runny batter. Add a little more milk if necessary.

Melt a tablespoon of butter in a frypan on medium heat. Pour a quarter of your batter into the pan to make your first pancake. When bubbles appear, flip the pancake over and cook the other side till golden brown.

Your tasty pancakes are now ready to be topped with your favorite fruit, nuts and maple syrup OR even a whole cooked breakfast (fried eggs, bacon, tomato, mushrooms and greens!).

Grandma's marvelous muffins

There's no rule saying you HAVE to have cereal for breakfast. How about a delicious, warm muffin instead? Make a batch of giant, low-sugar muffins at the start of the week, then simply defrost one each morning in the microwave for breakfast. Jackie's kids love this recipe that Grandma makes especially for them. Makes 12 regular or six large muffins:

2 cups self-rising flour

3 tbsp sugar

1 tsp baking powder

½ cup butter

1 cup milk

1 egg

1 tsp vanilla extract

Set your oven to 400F to warm up. Put all the dry ingredients into a large bowl. Melt the butter in a microwave-proof bowl and stir in the milk. Add the butter, milk, egg and vanilla to the dry ingredients and stir until it's just mixed. Divide evenly between muffin pans and bake in the center of the oven for 15 minutes.

This basic recipe can be adapted to use up pretty much anything. Add half a cup of your chosen fruit, or a teaspoon of your favorite spice or extract. Dad likes apple and cinnamon, Mom likes banana choc chip, Ali likes mixed berries and Liam loves a blob of jam in the middle!

Other great suggestions for a tasty breakfast alternative:

Super speedy scones – Snazzy snacks – Page 187
Ali's microwave scrambled eggs – Kid-friendly food – Page 159
Breakfast muffins – Bonus meals – Page 210
Couscous – Bonus meals – Page 211

Luscious lunches

Mexicana red lentil soup

This tasty soup has all the flavors of your favorite Mexican dinner and costs just cents to make. It's so quick and easy even the kids can make it, and dinner is on the table before you can say Arrrrreeeba!

1 cup red lentils

4 cups boiling water

1 x 14 oz can diced peeled tomatoes

3 stock cubes

½ tsp dried garlic powder or 2 cloves garlic, crushed

1 heaped tsp dried onion flakes

1 level tsp smokey paprika

1 level tsp ground cumin

1 level tsp ground ginger

1 level tsp ground coriander

¼-½ tsp chili flakes or hot chili powder (optional)

Put all the ingredients in to a large microwave-safe bowl and stir. Microwave on high for 6 minutes then stir thoroughly. Microwave on medium for 6 minutes then stir thoroughly again. If your lentils are not mushy, cook 3-4 minutes more on medium.

Serve with bread, tortillas or corn chips. If you're feeling extravagant, a dollop of sour cream and a sprinkle of fresh cilantro is a luxurious touch.

CONTRIBUTED BY: SUZY FREEME, ALSO KNOWN AS MIMI IN OUR FORUM. MIMI IS SUCH A LOVED MEMBER OF OUR FORUM THAT SHE ALSO HAS HER OWN SECTION IN OUR MONTHLY NEWSLETTER CALLED, 'COOKING WITH MIMI'.

Eat your words pastries

Many people have 'minor hurdles' who swear they will never eat leftovers. However, these baked delights will have them eating their words! They will make your leftovers smell so delicious they will be begging to eat them. NOTE: The egg is for glazing only so if you're hanging on to your eggs for your $21 Challenge week, don't panic, you don't HAVE to use it!

2 sheets puff pastry

1 tsp curry paste

Small bowl leftovers

Small quantity flour (optional)

Small quantity water or milk (optional)

1 egg, lightly beaten (optional)

Preheat your oven to 420F and defrost your pastry. To make your filling, put one cup of leftovers and a half teaspoon of curry paste into a bowl and mash it together. If you find your mix is a little too wet, add flour, or if it is too dry add a splash of milk or water.

Cut each of your defrosted sheets of pastry into four squares. Place one square on the palm of your hand so the middle of the square is in the center. Then place 1½ teaspoons of leftover mixture into the middle of the square. Fold one corner of the square over the top of the mix. Brush with the beaten egg. Then fold the next corner in, brush with egg, then the next and so on until you have made a little square parcel. Place onto a greased cookie tray. Repeat with the next parcel until all the ingredients are used up.

Bake in the oven for 25 minutes or until golden brown. Enjoy on its own or accompanied by a fresh salad. You can even serve these up for dinner with mashed potatoes, green vegetables and gravy. Yum!

Homemade sausage rolls

Kids love these in their lunchboxes and guys can't get enough of them either! These sausage rolls are delicious hot or cold and they are suitable for freezing. The best thing about this recipe is that you can sneak in all sorts of healthy vegetables that the kids won't know about! This recipe makes 36 mini sausage rolls but you can cut to whatever size you like. Larger size rolls can easily become a main dinner component when served with a salad and/or vegetables.

1 onion

Splash of oil

1 lb ground sausage

1 cup fresh breadcrumbs

2 tbsp ketchup

1 egg

Grated vegetables – try any combination of carrot, zucchini, pumpkin, sweet potato, corn or squash; they all taste great!

3 sheets puff pastry

Put your oven on to warm up at 400F. Heat the oil in a small frypan and gently fry the onion until golden, but not brown. Mix the other ingredients together in a bowl, add the onion and set aside.

Lay out your pastry sheets and cut each sheet into two rectangles. Divide the sausage mixture evenly between the six pastry rectangles. Shape the mixture into one long sausage down the middle of each sheet. Brush one long edge of the pastry with egg and roll up, then cut each roll to the required size. Place the rolls on a greased baking sheet, seam side down and brush the tops with egg. Bake for 15-20 minutes until the rolls are golden brown.

CONTRIBUTED BY: TRACEY SHUREY

Jackie's 'save the planet' soup

Did you know that a quarter of all food we buy is wasted? The problem is people don't know what to do with the last of their vegetables. As the name suggests, this soup is fantastic for saving money, vegetables AND the environment. It can be adapted to include pretty much anything you have on hand. In the past I have also added chopped zucchini, shredded Swiss chard, a handful of lentils, a can of tomatoes, chopped bacon for extra flavor; even the last few grains of rice or bits of pasta. Experiment as much as you like, you can't really go wrong!

This recipe serves eight so you get a week's worth of lunches plus a few extra to pop in the freezer for leftovers.

1 tbsp oil

2 onions, peeled and chopped

2 slices of bacon (if you have them)

2 oz peas or green beans (or both, if you're me!)

2 oz shredded cabbage (optional)

3 carrots, peeled and finely diced

3 celery sticks

1 large potato, peeled and finely diced

1 tbsp tomato paste

½ tsp mixed herbs

9 cups chicken stock (homemade or mixed from powder)

Salt and pepper

Heat the saucepan over medium heat. Fry the onion (and bacon if using) for a few minutes until golden. Add the rest of the vegetables along with the tomato paste, mixed herbs and chicken stock.

Turn up the heat until the soup is boiling, then reduce the heat and simmer gently for 30 minutes. Add salt and pepper to taste and enjoy!

If you want to freeze any for later, let the soup cool a little, then pour it into sealed containers. Once they have cooled completely, pop into the freezer where it will keep happily for three months.

Jackie's gourmet pies

You can turn pretty much anything into a pie with a couple of sheets of puff pastry and a pie maker! You can even make them ahead of time and freeze them in bulk for super fast lunches and snacks, which is really handy for $21 Challenge weeks. Add a selection of extra vegetables on the side and you have dinner! Jackie uses her trusty pie maker to turn all sorts of leftovers and goodies into delicious pies. Her favorite savory fillings include leftover bolognaise or chili con carne, leftover casserole or curry – beef stroganoff in particular makes a wonderful gourmet pie! If all you have on hand are a few leftover cooked veggies, you can still turn them into filling, tasty pies. Simply heat them through in a small frypan with a teaspoon or two of oil and a dash of curry powder before placing in your pie maker, or make a white or cheese sauce and mix the veggies in well. Use this mixture to fill your pies.

Even if you don't have a pie maker, you can still make individual snack-size pies. All you need is a muffin can, lightly greased of course! Use the rim of a cup or glass to cut circles out of puff pastry sheets. You need one circle to line the base and side of each pie and another to make the 'lid'. Fill the bases with your chosen filling, then gently pop the tops on. Use a fork to 'crimp' all around the edges and seal the pies. Bake at 400F for approximately 15 minutes, or until well risen and golden.

Emergency bread

In most households, running out of bread is considered an emergency! But it doesn't have to be the case. Our no kneading/no proofing/no fuss flat bread is here to the rescue. This is tasty enough that it just may become a treasured family favorite!

1 cup self-rising flour

1 egg

¾ cup water

½ cup milk

½ tsp salt

¼ tsp baking soda

Oil for frying

Put all your ingredients in a bowl and mix with an egg whisk until smooth. Let sit for 10 minutes, then heat up your frypan over medium heat. Once the pan is warm, put a splash of oil in it and spread it around. Pour around a quarter of the mixture into your pan. Soon bubbles will start to form across the top of the flat bread; keep cooking until these bubbles cover the entire surface and the color of the mixture changes slightly. Then turn the flat bread over with a spatula and cook the other side. Remove from your pan when ready and repeat the process until all the mixture is used. Now search around your kitchen for something tasty to go in it. Sweet or savory, the choice is yours!

Naomi's tasty toasties

Aussies love toasted sandwiches and Naomi from the Simple Savings team is a toasted sandwich genius! She has great recipes to suit everyone's tastes with all kinds of unexpected ingredients. She has made them out of jam, canned spaghetti, pineapple cubes, even chopped up chocolate bars!

All of the following combinations taste delicious and make two toasted sandwiches. Once you have tried one or two of the following recipes, get creative and make up some with your own recipe!

Meatlovers: Layer one tablespoon of chopped ham or leftover meat (or a slice of ham), one slice of cheese, one slice of red onion, salt and pepper on each sandwich.

Classy cheese: Mash two tablespoons of grated cheese with one and a half tablespoons of leftover veggies, a pinch of ginger, a pinch of ground coriander if you have some, salt and pepper.

Nearly Nutella: Mix one tablespoon of peanut butter with half a tablespoon of chocolate malted milk powder. Tastes like Nutella!

Popeye special: Mix three tablespoons of ricotta cheese and a small handful of baby spinach. While your bread is sitting on the toasted sandwich maker, distribute the mixture between sandwiches.

Cheese and mushroom: One sliced mushroom and two tablespoons of grated cheese or two slices of cheese. Spread ingredients across your sandwich and season with salt or pepper.

Spaghetti and corn: Mix two tablespoons of canned spaghetti and two tablespoons of canned corn. (Creamed corn is also nice but only use one tablespoon if you are using it.) A particular favorite to make after a night out on the town!

Pizza toastie: Mix two tablespoons of grated cheese with one clove of minced garlic (one teaspoon from jar), a pinch of dried rosemary and half a teaspoon of tomato paste.

Tuna and mayo: Mix one and a half tablespoons of tuna with two tablespoons of grated cheese and two finely chopped green onions. Use mayonnaise as a dipping sauce. Sounds bizarre but is yum!

Sweet apple: Mix one tablespoon of grated apple with one teaspoon of brown sugar. Kids love this one!

Caramel banana: Mash one banana with one teaspoon of butter and two teaspoons of brown sugar.

Spicy bean: Mix one tablespoon of baked beans with one teaspoon of chopped tomatoes and a dash of Tabasco sauce.

Surprise sandwiches!: Anything that is left over from last night's meal is fair game for a toasted sandwich experiment! Try spaghetti bolognaise, tuna pie, leftover veggies, taco meat – you'd be surprised how nice they can taste! It's also a good way to use up small, leftover portions. You can even freeze small portions like these and save them especially for surprise sandwiches when hunger strikes!

Marge's soulful tomato soup

This thick broth is a warm, gentle hug in a bowl! Serves 4.

4 cups water

2 tsp butter or oil

1 onion, finely chopped

1 tbsp crushed garlic (or 4 cloves, crushed)

6 medium ripe tomatoes

1 stalk celery, finely chopped

1-2 tsp sugar to taste

½ tsp salt and pepper

¼ cup tomato paste

2 cups chicken stock

Pinch chili powder

1-2 tbsp sour cream to taste (depends on tartness of tomatoes)

Boil the water in a medium sized saucepan. While waiting for it to to boil chop up your onions and crush the garlic. Heat your butter or oil in the frypan, pop in the onion and garlic and sauté gently until they are clear. Once your water is boiling in the other pan, it's time to remove the skins from your tomatoes. Do this by cutting the core from the tomatoes, dropping them in the boiling water for 30 seconds then putting them into a bowl of cold water for another 30 seconds. The skins will be loose enough to peel off. Easy! Next, roughly chop the tomatoes and put them into a large saucepan with all the ingredients except the sour cream. Heat the pan, stirring, until your soup is almost boiling. Then remove the pan from the heat and 'whiz' up your soup until nice and smooth, using a blender, food processor or stick blender. Stir in the sour cream to finish and serve steaming hot.

Sam's chicken soup

Fiona's son Sam absolutely loves his mom's homemade chicken soup. He literally begs for more! Here's how Fiona makes it. It's a wonderful way to use up every last scrap of last night's roast chicken too.

Be aware for those with allergies that this recipe contains peanut oil. It's the secret ingredient! Fiona can change the cooking times, vegetables or herbs and Sam doesn't notice. She doubts he would even notice if she swapped the chicken carcass for lamb bones! But, if she leaves out the peanut oil straight away he complains, 'What's wrong with the soup?'

Any veggies you have lurking in your fridge

Leftover roast chicken carcass

Celery leaves from one head

1 clove garlic

Small knob ginger

1 tbsp peanut oil

1 tsp salt

2 bay leaves (or a pinch of nutmeg)

1 tsp parsley

Roughly chop all your vegetables. Throw everything together in a pot and fill with enough water to cover the ingredients. Bring to boiling over a medium-high heat, then reduce heat and simmer for three hours to reduce a little. Leave to cool and strain into a container.

Sophie's best ever cheese scones

Who says you have to eat sandwiches for lunch? Anything goes during $21 Challenge week so if you run out of bread, no big deal! Make these tasty café style cheese scones instead. This recipe makes eight large scones. You can make them in bulk and freeze until required. These scones use just three ingredients and are the best we've ever tasted!

2 cups self-rising flour
2 cups grated cheese
1¼ cups milk

Start by preheating your oven to 400F. Combine the flour, cheese and any other seasonings you fancy (see variations) and mix well. Add the milk – the dough will be quite wet. Shape into small loaves or balls, sprinkle with extra cheese and bake for 10 minutes until well risen and crusty. Serve warm or cold.

Variations: You can add other flavors, such as cooked onion and bacon, chopped sun-dried tomatoes, chorizo, roasted bell peppers, feta and herbs. Try spreading some chutney or pesto over the top and adding a sprinkle of cheese before baking.

RECIPE COURTESY OF SOPHIE GRAY, DESTITUTEGOURMET.COM

For more terrific lunch ideas, check out some of these recipes too!

Jackie's versatile potato cakes – Divine dinners – Page 151
Café-style omelette – Divine dinners – Page 135
Liam's quick baked potatoes – Snazzy snacks – Page 183

Divine dinners

Chicken

Take a new look at the humble chook. From a simple sandwich to something far more elaborate, chicken is just so versatile, not to mention cheep cheep cheep!

Slow cooked French onion chicken

For chicken that just falls off the bone, try this easy crockpot dish. The onion soup gives this recipe a lovely flavor, slowly working its way through the chicken as it cooks. Magnifique!

1 tbsp oil for frying

1 onion, chopped

8-10 chicken drumsticks

1 x 14 oz can chopped tomatoes

1 package onion soup mix

1 tbsp soy sauce

½ cup water

Heat the oil in a small pan and fry the onion for a couple of minutes. While your onion is cooking, put the drumsticks into your crockpot. Combine your tomatoes, soup, soy sauce, water and cooked onion together in a bowl. Pour this mixture over your chicken, turning the meat to coat well. Cover and cook on low for eight hours until moist and tender. Delicious served with rice and steamed vegetables.

CONTRIBUTED BY: CAROL THOMPSON

Jackie's creamy chicken curry

The easiest curry you'll ever make and a great way to use up a can of soup! So mild and creamy even the little ones will love it.

Chicken pieces (enough for four people)

4 tbsp butter

1 large onion, chopped

2 tsp curry powder

1 tbsp flour

1 x 14 oz can condensed cream of chicken soup

9 oz sour cream

Salt and pepper

Preheat your oven to 350F for 10 minutes. Put your chicken in an ovenproof dish and cook for 30-40 minutes, turning once. Heat your butter until sizzling in a medium saucepan, and add your onion and curry powder, frying gently for a few minutes until tender. Add the flour, stir until all ingredients are combined and remove the pan from the heat. Add your soup, sour cream, salt and pepper to the pan and stir. Return the pan to the heat and keep stirring until your sauce thickens, then reduce heat and simmer for 2 minutes. Pour the sauce generously over your cooked chicken and serve with rice and vegetables.

One chicken – five dinners

This is the ultimate frugal dish. The secret to success is to cook a whole roast chicken, then see how many meals you can stretch out of it. Here's an example of how one chicken can be turned into five meals.

Enjoy freshly roasted chicken, then put all the leftovers in the fridge.

Then use some leftover meat in a pie – don't use it all though!

Add some more leftover meat to a healthy stir-fry.

Still got some left? Make chicken and salad sandwiches for lunch.

Finally, throw the whole carcass into a pot with some vegetables and turn it into nutritious soup or chicken stock, such as Sam's chicken soup in our luscious lunches section.

You get the idea, see what else you can come up with!

Sophie's crunchy peanut chicken with rice

This one-pan dish has all the comfort food qualities of risotto but has a bit more zing. Serve it with salad or green vegetables. Leftovers can be made into patties like risotto cakes.

1 tbsp oil

2 boneless, skinless chicken breasts, thinly sliced

1 onion, chopped

3 cloves garlic, crushed

1 x 14 oz can chopped tomatoes

¼ cup crunchy peanut butter

1 tbsp curry powder

3 cups chicken stock

1½ cups basmati or jasmine rice

Large pinch of thyme

½ tsp salt

Heat the oil in a large saucepan. Cook your chicken slices until sealed then set aside. Add your onion and garlic to the pan and cook till soft. Return your chicken to the pan and stir in your tomatoes, peanut butter, curry powder and thyme, mixing well to disperse the peanut butter through the mixture.

Add the chicken stock and bring to the boil. When your mixture is boiling, stir in the salt and rice. Return the mixture to boiling then cover and reduce the heat. Cook for 20 minutes on low then check to see if all the liquid is absorbed and your rice is cooked. Serve with a salad or green vegetables.

RECIPE COURTESY OF SOPHIE GRAY, DESTITUTEGOURMET.COM

Eggs

If you have an egg in the house, you have a meal in the house!

Light and golden veggie pie

This tasty self-crusting pie is an easy and effective way to use up all kinds of bits and pieces from your fridge or pantry.

4 eggs

2 cups milk

½ cup self-rising flour

1 tbsp melted butter

Added 'extras' of your choice, e.g. bacon and onion, tomato, tuna or whatever you have to hand.

1-2 cups grated, sliced or diced veggies

½ cup grated cheese for topping

Mix all your ingredients together in a large bowl until well combined. Pour into a greased casserole dish and bake for about 50 minutes at 350F until the vegetables are cooked through and the top is golden brown. Very tasty!

CONTRIBUTED BY: KATRINA MORGAN

Jackie's delicious salmon quiche

Another favorite among $21 Challengers, this recipe was given to Jackie years ago by her mother-in-law. She never dreamed how handy it would become! You can even use a smaller can of salmon if that's all you have available. It tastes just as good!

½ cup all-purpose flour

¼ tsp baking powder

4 eggs, beaten

2 cups milk

⅓ cup butter, melted

1 x 14 oz can pink salmon, drained

1 onion, chopped

½ cup grated cheese

1 tsp chives (optional)

Sift your flour and baking powder together into a large bowl. Make a well in the center of the flour and stir in your eggs, milk and butter. Add the salmon, onion and cheese, plus chives if using. Mix everything together until just combined and pour into a large, greased ovenproof dish. Cook at 350F for about 45 minutes until set. Serve with salad and/or steamed vegetables. Any leftovers are perfect for lunches the next day!

Café-style omelette

This recipe makes a delicious café-style omelette from just a few basic ingredients. Guaranteed to impress everyone at your table! Better still, you can adapt the recipe to include whatever bits and pieces need using up – cheese, chopped ham or cooked meat, fresh herbs, whatever you like, they're all delicious! This recipe makes one serving, simply repeat the process to make each omelette.

2 eggs
1 tbsp water
2 tsp butter or margarine
Salt and pepper

First, separate your eggs. To do this you need two bowls. Crack the egg over one of the bowls and, holding the yolk safely in one half of the shell, carefully pour all the 'white' into the bowl. Once you have caught all the egg white, pop the yolk into the second bowl. Repeat with the other egg. Add the water to the yolks, along with a sprinkle of salt and pepper, then mix. Using a hand whisk or electric whisk, beat the egg whites until they are stiff enough to stand up in small peaks. Gently fold the egg whites into the egg yolks and add any other ingredients you want to use at this point.

Heat the butter in a small frypan over medium heat. When your butter is bubbling, pour your mixture into the pan. Cook gently until set – you can check this by gently lifting up the edge of the omelette. If it's golden underneath, carefully turn over and finish off the other side. Remove from pan and 'fold' your omelette in half to serve. Delicious served with salad for a light meal or with added vegetables for a more substantial meal.

Meat

Jackie's homemade burgers (gluten-free)

If you're missing a fast food fix, don't blow your $21 Challenge budget buying burgers! Make your own healthier burgers for a fraction of the price. If you don't happen to have an egg in your house, don't panic. These burgers will work just as well without! This recipe makes four large or eight smaller burgers.

1 lb ground beef

½ small onion, chopped

Small bunch chopped parsley
(if you don't have it a pinch of mixed herbs will do)

1 egg

Oil for frying

Salt and pepper

Combine all your ingredients in a bowl and mix well. Divide your mixture into equal portions and shape into patties. The mixture will feel quite wet but don't worry, it sticks together well. Heat a little oil in a frypan over medium heat and place your burgers in the pan. Cook for around 7-10 minutes, turning occasionally until cooked through (e.g. no longer pink in the middle). These are delicious grilled or cooked on a BBQ too. If your $21 Challenge budget doesn't stretch to buying burger buns don't panic, these are just as good without them! Serve with salad, potato wedges and green vegetables.

Sophie's lonely sausage risotto

One sausage, four people, nothing much else defrosted. This risotto was an adventure that left us all smiling, it was so tasty, not to mention cheap, easy and filling. Desperation dining at its best! Jackie's family LOVES this recipe and finds it just as delicious with long grain rice if you don't happen to have arborio.

1 tbsp olive oil

1 onion, chopped

1 clove garlic, chopped

3 slices bacon

½ cups arborio rice

6½ cups chicken stock

1½ cups broccoli florets

1 cooked cold sausage, chopped into small pieces

½ cup grated cheese

Sauté the onion and garlic in the oil, add the bacon and sauté till soft. Stir in your arborio rice, stirring frequently until it is well coated in the flavorsome oil.

Add your stock a ladle at a time, stirring well and allowing the stock to be absorbed before each addition. When a quarter of the stock has been added, toss in your broccoli and the sausage. Continue adding stock and stirring until your rice has swelled and thickened and the risotto is a creamy texture.

Stir in the grated cheese and serve immediately to an appreciative group. Delicious accompanied with green vegetables – or, if you're Jackie's youngest son, warmed up for breakfast the next day!

RECIPE COURTESY OF SOPHIE GRAY, DESTITUTEGOURMET.COM

Kate's thymely tomato casserole

This recipe has Fiona's all 'thyme' favorite combination:- rosemary, thyme, garlic, salt and tomato. They taste so good together! It was also one of the first combinations Fiona used to trick her new boyfriend Matt into thinking she could cook. Luckily that was many years ago and in the years that followed Fiona really DID learn how to cook. But, this is Kate's recipe not Fiona's, so let's get on with it!

One of the great things about this recipe is that it is very flexible. You can use all types of meat or create a tasty vegetarian meal.

1-1½ lb diced beef, lamb, chuck steak or chicken

1 tbsp flour

1 tbsp oil

1 large onion, chopped (or 1 small onion and 1 leek)

3 cloves garlic, crushed

1 tsp each dried rosemary and thyme

1 stick celery, finely chopped

2 carrots, peeled and sliced

7 oz mushrooms, sliced

2 green onions (optional)

2 x 14 oz cans tomatoes (or 6 fresh tomatoes, finely chopped)

2 tbsp tomato paste

½ cup beef stock

½ cup white wine

1 tbsp fresh parsley

Salt and pepper to taste

Preheat your oven to 320-340F. Coat your meat in flour then brown on medium-high heat. Put meat in a large casserole dish.

Saute your onions, garlic, celery, carrot and herbs in the pan until soft, then add them to your casserole dish along with your mushrooms, green onions, tomatoes, paste, stock, wine, parsley, salt and pepper. Stir well to combine everything.

Cook, covered in the oven for 1 hour for chicken or 1½ hours for beef or lamb. Uncover and cook for a further 20-30 minutes to thicken your sauce.

Serve with mashed potatoes and beans or rice and green salad.

No meat? No worries!

If you have run out of meat, you can replace the meat with 2-3 cans of chickpeas, butter beans or canellini beans (or a combination).

Preheat your oven to 320-340F. Sautee your onions, garlic, carrot, celery and herbs. Pop these in your casserole dish, sprinkle the flour over the top and stir through. Add all remaining ingredients to your dish, including your beans, then cook, covered in the oven for 45 minutes. Remove the lid and cook a further 20 minutes until sauce thickens.

Kate's bacon and red wine casserole

This warming casserole is so rich and flavorsome your family will think Martha Stewart herself must be hiding somewhere in the kitchen! The combination of celery, bay leaves and parsley in this recipe is a traditional French seasoning, while bacon and wine are the key ingredients to creating this delicious sauce. Serves 4-6.

1-1½ lb diced beef, lamb or chuck steak

1 tbsp flour

1 tbsp oil

2 large onions, chopped (or 6-8 small pickling onions, quartered)

2-3 green onions (optional)

3 cloves garlic, crushed

1-2 tsp dried oregano

1-2 tsp dried thyme

2 bay leaves (dried or fresh)

1-2 slices bacon, chopped

7 oz mushrooms, whole, sliced or finely chopped

2 carrots, sliced or finely chopped

1 tbsp fresh parsley, chopped

1 stick celery, finely chopped

Peel of ½ orange (optional), use whole pieces not grated

3 tbsp tomato paste

1-1½ cups beef stock

1 cup red wine (or 2 tbsp wine vinegar plus ¾ cup vegetable stock)

1 tbsp Worcestershire sauce or balsamic vinegar

Salt and pepper to taste

Roll the diced meat in a little flour to coat. Heat the oil in a frypan, add your meat and stir quickly until brown all over, then put the meat in a large casserole dish for later. Pop the frypan back on to the heat and throw in the onions. Cook for a few minutes until soft, then add your green onions, garlic, oregano, thyme and bay leaves to the frypan. Stir and cook for another 2-3 minutes and then put the whole mix into the casserole dish. Next add your bacon to the frypan, cook gently for a few minutes and then put it in your casserole dish.

Add the rest of your prepared vegetables to the casserole dish. Mix the rest of your ingredients together in a bowl. Add your mix to the casserole dish and stir everything together. Cook, covered in a moderate oven (320-340F) for 1 hour 20 minutes (unless using chuck steak, in which case cook for 2 hours at 300F). Stir well, remove the orange peel and cook uncovered for a further 20 minutes at 350F.

Serve your casserole with mashed potatoes or pasta for a dish that everyone will love.

One pot bonus

If you would like to turn this into an easy 'one pot' meal, just throw two cups of diced potato into your casserole dish with the rest of the vegetables.

Star Wars hotpot

This recipe comes from *The Blue Peter Book of Gorgeous Grub*, which Jackie became the proud owner of as a young whippersnapper growing up in England. The recipe got its name because it was invented at the same time as the original Star Wars movie (which shows her age!).

1 tbsp oil

1 lb sausages, cut into one inch slices

1 medium onion, chopped

6 oz bacon, chopped

1 x 8 oz can baked beans

1 small can sweet corn kernels

1 large can tomatoes, chopped

1 bay leaf

Salt and pepper

2 large potatoes, peeled and thinly sliced

½ cup grated cheese (optional)

Preheat your oven to 300F. Heat the oil in a frypan and add your sausages, onion and bacon and brown gently. Pop the mixture in your casserole dish and add your beans, corn, tomatoes and bay leaf then season well with salt and pepper. Mix well to combine everything then top with the sliced potatoes. Cover and cook for about 2½ hours. Remove the lid, turn the heat up to 375F and cook for another 30 minutes to brown the potatoes. Throw some grated cheese on top and return to the oven for a few minutes until the cheese is golden brown.

For other meat recipes go to:

Lasagna – Divine dinners – Page 145
Kate's lifesaving beef – Kid-friendly food – Page 162

Pasta

Tomato and garlic pasta sauce

There's no need to buy jars of pasta sauce once you know how to make your own! This recipe is delicious and will compliment any type of pasta. It freezes well too, so you will always have a meal on hand. Just pour over pasta and enjoy!

2 onions

4 cloves garlic

2 carrots

A few sticks celery

1 tbsp olive oil

1 tbsp butter

2 x 14 oz cans tomatoes

Put all your vegetables except the tomatoes in a food processor and 'whiz' until chopped superfine.

Drizzle the oil into a saucepan and add a knob of butter. Add the vegetable mixture and cook on low heat for 15 minutes.

Add tomatoes, salt and pepper and simmer for a further 30 minutes.

Serve over the top of cooked pasta, accompanied by steamed vegetables or a tasty salad.

CONTRIBUTED BY: JACQUI ANTONIAZZI

Pasta with chicken, white wine and cream

Enjoy a little luxury during $21 Challenge week with this 'made in minutes' pasta dish. A splash of white wine gives this creamy dish a touch of decadence, just like you'd find in an Italian restaurant!

2 tbsp oil

1 onion, chopped

2 tsp garlic, crushed

½ green onion, chopped

7 oz cooked chicken, shredded

White wine

1 cup cream

Parmesan cheese

Chicken stock powder

4 cups cooked pasta (penne or spiral works best)

Heat the oil in a frypan over medium heat. Sauté your onion, garlic and green onions until the onion has caramelized, being careful not to burn.

Add your cooked, shredded chicken and mix through until the meat is well coated with the spicy sautéed ingredients.

Throw in two good splashes of wine and simmer, stirring until the liquid has reduced. Add your cream, Parmesan and two pinches of chicken stock for extra flavor.

Allow the cream to thicken before stirring through the cooked pasta.

Serve with a side salad or green vegetables.

CONTRIBUTED BY: JULIE DEVERY. RECIPE COURTESY OF LA FIESTA.

Lasagna

Lasagna makes a little meat go a long way. The great thing about this family favorite is you can use cheaper generic brands and they'll taste just as good as the more expensive ingredients. This recipe makes good use of any jars of pasta sauce you have lurking in your pantry.

1 tbsp oil

1 lb ground beef

1 jar pasta sauce

1 x 14 oz can chopped tomatoes

1 tbsp butter

1½ tbsp flour

1 cup milk

Lasagna noodles (fresh or dried)

1 cup grated cheese

Heat your oil in a saucepan on medium-high heat. Add the ground beef and keep stirring until it's brown all over. Add your pasta sauce and tomatoes. Bring to the boil, then turn down the heat and simmer for 10 minutes. Set aside to cool while you make your white sauce. To do this, melt your butter in a saucepan and add the flour. Mix to a soft, doughy ball, ensuring the sauce doesn't burn. Slowly add one cup of milk and stir constantly until you have a smooth mixture. Take the pan off the heat and let it cool.

Grease a large, deep baking dish and layer the ingredients in the following order: meat, lasagna noodles, white sauce, cheese; then repeat, ending with cheese. Cook in the oven for about 50-60 minutes at 350F.

Super serving suggestion: If you have some fresh garlic, you have to try this awesome side dish to go with your lasagna! Chop up some tomatoes, green beans, mushrooms, three cloves of garlic and a couple of sprigs of parsley. Lightly fry them together with a little oil in a frypan, stirring frequently until they start to brown. Then drizzle a bit of vinegar on top and stir it through.

CONTRIBUTED BY: ELIZABETH BLYTH

Lite and creamy veggie pasta

Jackie came across this recipe years ago in a magazine ad for Nestle's Carnation Evaporated Milk and has been enjoying it ever since. It's a great way to use up extra zucchini and is also lower in fat than most cream-based pasta dishes.

> *11 oz spaghetti or pasta*
>
> *1 tbsp oil*
>
> *3 cups sliced vegetables (I like to use red bell peppers, zucchini and mushrooms but use whatever you have on hand)*
>
> *1 x 12 oz can low-fat evaporated milk*
>
> *1 tbsp cornstarch*
>
> *1 tbsp mustard (wholegrain is best)*
>
> *1 cup grated cheese*
>
> *Salt and pepper*

Cook and drain your pasta according to directions on the box. Heat the oil in a large pan, add your sliced veggies and cook for 2 minutes. Add the evaporated milk, cornstarch and mustard to the pan and bring to the boil, stirring all the time. Stir your cheese into the bubbling mixture and simmer until it has melted. Remove from heat, toss through your cooked pasta and season with salt and pepper. A filling meal on its own or accompanied with salad and green vegetables.

Cheesy pasta bake

Why buy expensive pasta bake sauces when you can make your own? This easy version can be adapted to use up whatever you have available and tastes so much nicer than the stuff you buy.

11 oz pasta of your choice

1 x 14 oz can chopped tomatoes

1 tbsp melted butter

1 tbsp flour

2 cups chopped, cooked vegetables of your choice

3 slices ham, finely chopped (optional)

1 cup grated cheese

2 eggs

1 cup milk

Start by cooking your pasta according to the directions on the box. When it's done, grease a large casserole dish and spoon your cooked, drained pasta into it.

Pour in your canned tomatoes and butter, then sprinkle the flour on top and stir through. Layer your chopped vegetables and ham, followed by a sprinkling of grated cheese. Yum!

Next, grab a bowl and beat your egg and milk. Pour this mixture over the top of your ingredients in the casserole dish and bake at 350F for 20-25 minutes until set.

Serve with shredded lettuce or some big, fat lettuce leaves. Just like store bought – only better!

CONTRIBUTED BY: JENNIFER GEORGE

Shelley's superb pasta sauces

If you have some pasta in the cupboard then you have the makings of a gourmet meal. You'll be amazed how you can convert some garlic, onion and odds and ends from your kitchen to make a delicious sauce.

We challenged Simple Savings staffer Shelley to invent some new divine pasta sauces to show people how flexible and tasty pasta can be.

Set your pasta cooking before you start making your sauce. We estimate you will need about 13-14 oz of dried pasta. Serves 4.

Mediterranean Verde: Saute 2-4 cloves of crushed garlic and one chopped onion in 1 tablespoon of oil on medium heat in a large frypan. Add 4 oz fresh or frozen spinach, parsley, 12 green olives, a dash of olive oil, 2 tablespoons of lime juice and 2 cups of mixed veggies and stir. Mix in your drained pasta. Serve with your favorite cheese and almond slivers sprinkled across the top. Delicious!

Citrus twist: Saute 2-4 cloves of crushed garlic and one chopped onion in 1 tablespoon of oil on medium heat in a large frypan. Add ½ cup drained artichokes and douse with 2 tablespoons of lemon juice and the zest of one lemon plus any herbs you have to hand (parsley, basil, shallots, chives, oregano – fresh is best). Mix in your drained pasta. Sprinkle with Parmesan cheese and serve with a side salad. Great either hot or cold!

Nice le noci: Saute 2-4 cloves of crushed garlic and one chopped onion in 1 tablespoon of oil on medium heat in a large frypan. Add 2 oz of chopped nuts (walnuts, almonds, cashews, brazil nuts or whatever you have in the pantry), a bunch of fresh parsley or herbs, add some chili and some extra olive oil so that it is glistening. Season with salt and pepper then stir through hot pasta. Serve with grated cheese and a squirt or two of lemon juice and a green salad. Buon appetito!

Porky bumpkin: Heat a large frypan on medium. Add 1 tablespoon of oil and saute 2-4 cloves of crushed garlic, one chopped onion, 5 oz chopped bacon (ham or spam), 9 oz finely chopped pumpkin (or squash, zucchini, red bell peppers or mushrooms) and a teaspoon of dried herbs. Add the drained pasta and ½ stick of butter then stir through. Sprinkle with salt, pepper and Parmesan cheese to serve.

Spring sensation: Saute 2-4 cloves of crushed garlic and one chopped onion in 1 tablespoon of oil on medium heat in a large frypan. Add 1½ cups fresh or frozen peas, 2 cups of finely chopped vegetables (such as sweet potato, carrot or fresh/frozen corn). Once the vegetables are cooked, stir through your drained pasta. Dress and serve with a handful of fresh mint leaves and crumbly fetta cheese. Fantastic with a glass of white wine.

All year Christmas cheer: Heat a large frypan on medium. Add 1 tablespoon of oil and saute 2-4 cloves of crushed garlic, one chopped onion, 5 oz chopped bacon (ham or chicken) and 2 whole cloves. Once the meat is cooked, remove the cloves and add 4 tablespoons of shredded coconut, 1 cup cranberries (or other dried fruits), some slivered almonds, a generous blob of maple syrup and a sprinkling of ground allspice. Stir through your drained pasta and garnish with fresh mint leaves to serve.

Potatoes

Baked potatoes

This recipe is the perfect way to use up leftover bolognaise, chili con carne, tuna casserole – any leftovers will do! Use whatever you have on hand as a filling, even grated cheese and tomato relish works great.

Use one medium to large sized potato per person. Scrub your potatoes, pierce the skin half a dozen times with a fork and microwave for around five minutes, until cooked through.

Cut a slit in the top of each potato and spoon out some of the potato. Place the potatoes close together in an ovenproof dish.

Spoon your chosen filling over the top of each potato. Add grated cheese or a dollop of salsa for spicier dishes.

Bake at 350F for around 20 minutes until the filling is heated through and the cheese is golden and bubbling.

Serve with salad or mixed veggies for a tasty, balanced meal.

CONTRIBUTED BY: JUDITH LONG

Jackie's versatile potato cakes

These versatile potato cakes can be made as small or large as you like and adapted to use up whatever leftovers you have – cooked corned beef, bacon, smoked fish, the list goes on and on. Of course it's a great way to use up leftover mashed potato too! You can make these ahead of time and refrigerate until ready to cook.

2-3 cups mashed potato, left to cool

12 oz corned beef, smoked fish or whatever, cut into bite size pieces

2 eggs, beaten

1-2 tbsp wholegrain mustard (optional)

1 cup all-purpose flour

Combine the meat, eggs and mustard and season to taste. Add your mashed spuds and mix all ingredients until they are well combined. Shape the mixture into patties, coat each one with flour and set aside. Heat up a large frypan and pour in enough oil to shallow fry the patties over medium heat. Fry for a few minutes on each side until heated through and golden brown.

You can add whatever you like to jazz up your patties – freshly chopped chives or curry powder works well. It doesn't seem to matter what I put in, my family always love them! These are delicious served with lightly steamed broccoli, green beans and sliced carrots. Even better with a dollop of chutney on the side!

Spicy Mexican bean pie

This 'pie' is a fun and interesting way to turn everyday mashed spuds into something special. So easy and economical to make, and tasty too!

4 cups mashed potato, left to cool

Olive oil

1 medium onion, diced

2 x 14 oz cans chopped tomatoes

1 package taco seasoning (*or homemade, see below)

1 x 14 oz can kidney beans, rinsed and drained

Pinch of mixed dried herbs

½ cup grated cheese

Preheat your oven to 350F. Grease a medium casserole dish, then use three cups of your mashed potato to line the bottom and sides. Make sure you leave one cup of potato for the pie crust. Heat a good splash of olive oil in a frypan, add your onion and fry for a few minutes over medium heat. Put your tomatoes, taco seasoning, kidney beans, herbs and cooked onions into a bowl and mix together well. Spoon the mixture into your potato pie shell. Cover the top of the dish with the last cup of mashed potato and sprinkle grated cheese over the top. Bake in the oven for about 20 minutes. This dish tastes great with a simple salad of lettuce, grated carrot, finely sliced cucumber and tomato.

CONTRIBUTED BY: KIM BROOKS

Tip: If you don't have ready-made taco seasoning you can easily make your own. Put one teaspoon each of paprika, ground cumin, chili powder and oregano in a bowl with half a teaspoon each of sugar and salt. Stir to combine and add to the recipe until required taste is achieved.

Cheesy potato pie for one

Don't let the title fool you. You can adapt this recipe to use up whatever veggies you have on hand and it will easily feed more than one person.

Small amount of oil or butter to sauté

1 onion, finely chopped

1 slice bread

1 egg, beaten

Salt and pepper

¼ tsp paprika

1 small potato, grated (peeled or unpeeled, you choose)

¼ cup grated cheese

Preheat your oven to 400F. Heat the oil or butter in a pan over medium heat and sauté the onion for a few minutes until soft. Wet your bread under a tap, gently squeeze out any excess water and tear into small pieces. Put the bread into a mixing bowl followed by the cooked onion. Add the egg, salt, pepper and paprika to the bowl and mix. Finally, add the grated potato and cheese and mix until combined with the other ingredients. Grease or spray a large Pyrex dish or small ramekins. Fill the dish with your potato mixture and make sure you leave half an inch of space at the top, so the mix doesn't bubble over. Cook for 20-25 minutes until lightly browned on top.

Serving suggestion: We love this dish served with a salad of sliced mushroom, grated zucchini, fresh dill from the yard and a little extra chopped onion. Add a simple dressing of lemon juice, olive oil and a pinch of salt and pepper and drizzle lightly over the top. Delicious!

CONTRIBUTED BY: JO WILSON

Rice

Rice and risottos of all types are great during Challenge weeks. They are filling and flavorsome and many can be made from leftovers or from very few ingredients.

Magnificent mushroom and Parmesan risotto

This super fast meal requires just a few ingredients to make. Grab those mushrooms out of your fridge and turn them into something fantastic!
If you have Parmesan cheese it's great for some extra bite but ordinary grated cheese will do.

1 tbsp butter

1 onion, diced

4-6 large mushrooms, sliced

2 cups rice, pre-cooked in vegetable stock

Parmesan cheese, grated

Heat your tablespoon of butter in a frypan over medium heat. Once the butter is sizzling, sauté your onion and mushrooms for a few minutes until soft. Remove the pan from the heat and add your veggies to the cooked rice. Return to the heat until piping hot and sprinkle with the Parmesan. So easy!

Super serving suggestion: If you happen to have some spinach in your freezer or in your garden, cook separately and stir through at the end for some extra greens.

CONTRIBUTED BY: KIRBY CHESNEY

Hearty vegetarian risotto

This meat-free meal is rather like chili con carne, without the chili or the carne! Kids love it too; just don't tell them it's good for them!

1-2 tbsp olive oil

1 clove garlic, crushed

Cumin seeds, or any other spices you have to hand

1½ cups uncooked rice

1 x 14 oz can diced tomatoes

1 large can kidney beans, rinsed and drained

1 heaped tsp stock powder dissolved in one cup water

Extra water

Grated cheese

Sour cream (optional)

Heat oil in a large pan and gently cook garlic and spices for a couple of minutes. Add the rice to the pan, mixing in well enough to coat it in the garlic and spices and cook for another minute. Stir in your tomatoes, kidney beans and stock. Cover and cook on low heat until your rice is cooked and a little creamy. Check the pan regularly and stir in half a cup of water each time – this keeps the rice from drying out and sticking to the pan (you may need to do this 4-5 times). Once your rice is cooked through, serve with sour cream, grated cheese and salad or vegetables.

NB: The sour cream was added later just because we had some in the fridge, but you don't really need it, it's still yummy without it!

CONTRIBUTED BY: KATH CORBEN

Tuna

These mouth watering recipes magically turn a humble can of tuna into a filling meal that will easily feed a whole family. A great way to use up all sorts of other 'bits and pieces' too!

Naomi's cheesy tuna pie

This recipe has become a $21 Challenge classic among Simple Savings members. It's a brilliant way to use up spare crackers in your pantry. It's divine for dinner and delicious when eaten cold for lunch the next day. So quick to make too – perfect after a busy day!

> *2 largish handfuls of crackers*
>
> *1 cup milk*
>
> *1 onion, diced*
>
> *3 eggs*
>
> *2 sprigs fresh parsley*
>
> *1 cup grated cheese*
>
> *1 large can tuna*

Break your crackers up into a blender and pour the milk over them. Add your onion, eggs, parsley and grated cheese. Drain the tuna well and add to the other ingredients. Blend everything together until well combined. If you don't have a blender, you can put all the ingredients in a large bowl and build up those muscles with a potato masher to break up the lumps and bind the ingredients together. It's worth the effort! Cook in a greased pie or baking dish at 350F for 30-40 minutes. This tastes lovely with just about any salad or vegetable dish!

CONTRIBUTED BY: NAOMI BRUVELS

Tuna, tomato and bell pepper sauce

A pasta sauce with a difference! This is the perfect example of how you can create a special recipe from basic ingredients during a $21 Challenge week. Serve this with your favorite pasta. If you don't have pasta, try serving it with rice, noodles, potatoes or crusty bread.

Small can tuna in oil (plain or flavored)

1 onion, chopped

1 green pepper, sliced

1 clove garlic

1 x 14 oz can tomato puree (or you can puree a can of tomatoes)

1 tbsp tomato paste

½ cup white wine

Olives (optional)

2 tbsp chopped parsley or basil

Black pepper to taste

Open your can of tuna and drain it over a large saucepan so that it catches all the oil – don't pour it down the drain! Heat the oil in your pan over medium heat. Sauté the onion, pepper and garlic for a few minutes until the onion is tender. Stir in your tomato puree, tomato paste and wine and cook a few minutes more. Add your tuna to the pot and stir gently for a final five minutes. Serve with a crisp lettuce salad and garnish with olives and fresh parsley for a finishing touch.

CONTRIBUTED BY: JUDITH LONG

Kid-friendly food

As a rule, kids love taking part in the $21 Challenge. They enjoy helping Mom and Dad sort out the pantry and finding ways to use up ingredients. Kids are not scared to experiment with food, so allow them a little creative license when coming up with suggestions – you may find their ideas give way to some new family favorites! The $21 Challenge even encourages 'fussy' kids to eat! They love to help Mom and Dad 'beat' the Challenge and often become more willing to try all sorts of new dishes. The more input you allow, the more likely they are to give things a go – and like them.

However, there are always exceptions to the rule and not every child is so willing to experiment. If your child is used to frozen pizzas and chicken nuggets for dinner and is suddenly expected to eat 'proper food', they could get a shock! They may also object to having their usual dinner routine tossed out of the window, but there are ways you can make the transition easier. Some tried and true $21 Challenge tips for kids include:

1. Get your child to at least try his/her meal. If they try it and still don't like it, fair enough, but they won't know unless they try.

2. Teach them how important it is to you that they eat properly. 'I have made you all this lovely food because I care about you, so you can grow big and strong and healthy. It really hurts my feelings when you won't even try it for me.'

3. Hide the veggies! If Jackie put carrot, zucchini or onion on her kids' plates they wouldn't dream of touching it. BUT – if she adds them to a ground beef dish and gives them a quick whiz with a stick blender, they devour the whole thing! It's a great way to use up all the little bits of vegetables that your child won't normally eat.

Even if they are absolutely hell-bent on refusing what you put in front of them, do not despair! All you need is to keep a slice of bread and an egg on hand to smooth things over:

Ali's microwave scrambled eggs

Jackie's 10-year-old is an expert at making scrambled eggs in the microwave. Here's how he does it, in his own words:

2 eggs

A bit of parsley

¼ cup milk

¼ cup grated cheese

Toast

Butter

First, crack the eggs into a bowl. Tear up the parsley a bit and chuck it over the eggs. Add the milk and cheese, then stir. Put in the microwave on high for 45 seconds then stir. Cook for another 25 seconds and stir again. Zap one more time for around 15 seconds and stir. Make the toast and butter it. Put the scrambled eggs on top. Perfection!

Boiled egg and toast fingers

For perfect soft boiled eggs every time, bring enough water to cover the eggs to the boil. Gently lower your eggs into the water and set your timer for six minutes. Start cooking your toast. When it is done, butter it and then slice into fingers. When the timer goes off, remove your eggs and run them under cold water. Serve in an egg cup with yummy buttery toast fingers.

Egg in a nest

To make everyday eggs really egg-citing, try this! Put a frypan on medium heat. Butter both sides of a slice of bread then use a glass to 'stamp' a hole out of the middle of the bread. Set this aside. Put the bread in your pan then crack a raw egg into the hole in the middle. Add your leftover round piece to the pan too. Cook until golden brown then flip. Cook until golden on both sides and serve hot. Only takes about 10 minutes per serving and is guaranteed to make your kids smile.

French toast

Kids love French toast! This recipe will make 4-6 slices. For a quick tummy pleaser, simply beat two eggs in a large bowl with two tablespoons of milk. Heat one tablespoon of butter in a frypan over medium heat. Dip each slice of bread into the eggy mix and coat on both sides. Place into the frypan one slice at a time and cook until golden on the underside. Flip over and cook the other side. To serve, enjoy on its own or sprinkle with cinnamon, honey, whatever you like! You can even freeze any cold leftover French toast in single layers and simply reheat in your toaster as required for a super speedy breakfast or snack. Couldn't be easier!

Mouthwatering homemade pizza

A great way to use up all sorts of odds and ends such as the last piece of ham or leftover bacon is having homemade pizza for dinner. Making your own crusts is really easy. This recipe makes four delicious pizzas and they freeze like a dream. A big help during Challenge week! Try it!

2 tsp dried yeast
1 tsp sugar
1½ cups warm water
3 cups all-purpose flour
1 tsp salt
3 tbsp olive oil
Tomato paste
Grated cheese
Herbs
Favorite toppings

Mix the yeast, sugar and warm water together and stand for 5 minutes in a warm place. Place flour, salt and oil in a large bowl. Make a well in the center and add the yeast mixture. Stir with a butter knife to form a soft dough. Knead dough for 5 minutes on a floured surface then place the dough in a greased bowl and cover with plastic wrap. Stand in a warm spot for 45 minutes or until doubled in size. While the dough is rising, prepare your toppings and put your oven on to 400-420F to heat up. Be sure to ask the kids what they would like on their pizza – they are more likely to eat it then and pizzas are so flexible virtually everything tastes good. Who knows, you may come up with a completely new taste sensation, such as peanut butter, golden raisins, coconut and chicken pizza! Divide your ball of dough into four equal portions and roll out on a floured surface. Add your toppings, starting with tomato paste at the bottom and finishing with the grated cheese. Bake on a flat oven tray for 20-25 minutes.

CONTRIBUTED BY: TRACEY GALEA

Kate's lifesaving beef

This recipe is guaranteed to become an indispensable addition to your cooking repertoire. It has everything! For starters it's easy to make, tastes wonderful and is full of hidden veggies. Best of all though, this recipe makes enough for two or three meals. So it will save you time. Give it a go.

2 medium carrots, roughly chopped

2 medium onions, roughly chopped

2 zucchini, roughly chopped

1-2 cups roughly chopped mixed vegetables (the more variety the better, e.g. broccoli, mushroom, cauliflower, spinach, celery, cabbage, even a little pumpkin or sweet potato)

1 tbsp oil

2 cloves garlic, crushed

2 lb ground beef

1 beef stock cube

1 cup of red wine (optional)

2 jars tomato pasta sauce (or 2 cans chopped tomatoes)

2 tbsp tomato paste

1-2 tsp dried oregano

1-2 tsp dried basil (or 3 fresh sprigs, finely chopped)

2 bay leaves

Fresh parsley if you have it

Put all your vegetables in a food processor or blender and chop until super fine. Warm your oil in a large saucepan over a medium-high heat. Brown your garlic and meat in the saucepan. Add the pureed uncooked vegetables to the pan. Add any remaining ingredients and bring to the boil. Reduce the heat, cover and simmer gently for 1-2 hours, stirring regularly. Enjoy half tonight and store the rest for later.

Making a second and third meal

Kate's lifesaving beef is brilliant because you can turn it into a whole new meal. Try some of these:

Spaghetti bolognaise: Stir through a little ketchup just before serving for a sweeter taste and sprinkle with grated cheddar or Parmesan.

Lasagna: Layer with lasagna noodles and white sauce, then sprinkle the top with grated cheese.

Pies and pastries: Simply cook up a few extra vegetables – mushroom, peas or diced potato – then mix with the meat and use as a pie filling, or wrap in filo pastry.

Shepherd's pie: Mix a large handful of peas with your meat mixture and place in the bottom of a pie dish. Microwave/steam four peeled potatoes and mash with milk and butter, then place on top of the meat. Cook your pie at 350F for 30-40 minutes.

Nachos: Mix a little curry paste, and/or sweet chili sauce through your beef along with some kidney beans and serve over the top of corn chips with cheese, avocado, tomato, salsa and sour cream.

Tortillas and tacos: Use plain beef or nachos beef (see above) and serve on tortillas or in taco shells with chopped tomato, cheese, lettuce, avocado, corn kernels, sour cream and salsa.

Toasted sandwiches: Simply add a little tomato or barbecue sauce and cheddar for a super easy meal, or serve on toast.

Crafty platters

One of the Lippey's favorite dinners are legendary snack platters that the kids have made with their wild imaginations; such as Sam's Temple to the God of Bread, Tristan's Mandarin Mountain and Jacqui's Magnificent Morsels. Everyone has an absolute ball making and eating them. First they gather the ingredients together and chop, slice and prepare the food with lots of laughter. Then, when it's time to decorate the platters, the kids and their personalities take over. It's a lot of fun! Whoever said kids should never play with their food was WRONG!

The key to making a nutritious, well balanced meal is to ensure half the snacks are fresh fruit and vegetables, a quarter are protein-based and a quarter are carbohydrates. To make it easier for you, here is a list of foods you could put on your platters. After your main meal, if you feel like something sweet, why not put together a dessert platter?

Fruit and vegetables (half of your platter)

Long carrot sticks • thin celery strips • cauliflower florets • broccoli 'trees' • fresh green beans • cleaned mushrooms – decorate with smiley faces (golden raisins, ketchup, cream cheese) • pumpkin or sweet potato wedges (p245) • strips of bell peppers (red, green and yellow together look brilliant) • cherry tomatoes • green or black olives (try the ones stuffed with cheese or fish) • cucumber rounds • sliced canned beets • pieces of fresh fruit (cut up apples, mandarins, strawberries, kiwi fruit, melons) • dried fruit (apricots, dates, cranberries, apple rings, golden raisins, raisins) • four bean salad (p225) • Fiona's gluten and dairy-free veggie patties (p250) • cold roasted eggplant • shredded lettuce • sundried tomatoes • sliced avocado • small corn cobs • asparagus spears • fresh parsley and mint.

Protein (quarter of your platter)

Hard boiled eggs, peeled and halved • cheese cut into wedges • assorted nuts (cashews are a favorite) • cold meat cuts (try leftover steak sprinkled with salt) • fish, tuna or salmon from a can • smoked oysters or other seafood • snazzed up leftovers (sprinkle with Parmesan) • homemade sausage rolls (p120) • mini Jackie's homemade burgers (p136) • yogurt pots (p188) • peanut butter (also great for joining bits of food together) • assorted dips (p180) such as hummus, French onion, guacamole.

Carbohydrates (quarter of your platter)

Chips • pretzels • corn chips • triangles of heated tortillas or other flat breads • bagels • rice crackers • savory crackers • sweet plain cookies • fresh popcorn (p187) • pasta leftovers • scalloped potatoes (p224) • creamed corn fritters (p208) • rice paper rolls (p198)

Dessert

Dried fruit (apricots, dates, golden raisins, cranberries or glace cherries) • assorted nuts (cashews, almonds, brazil nuts, or choc-coated) • segments of sliced fresh fruit (watermelon, cantaloupe, honeydew melon, papaya, strawberries, kiwi fruit, blueberries, peaches and plums) • gourmet cheese wedges • mini pancakes (p116) • golden raisin muffins (p172) • fruity yogurt muffins (p182) • pikelets (p186) • tutti frutti muffins (p227) • plain sweet cookies (p176) • easy chocolate slice (p181) • mini granola bars (p184) • freshly made popcorn (p187) • sprinkled with powdered sugar • snowdrops (p206).

Try adding a sweet sauce in the center of your platter like melted marshmallows, honey yogurt, melted chocolate, rich chocolate sauce (p212), custard, caramel topping (p206), cream or condensed milk.

McMommy's

Just because fast food is off limits during $21 Challenge weeks, the kids don't have to miss out on their favorite treats. Simply make your own! Simple Savings member Michelle Leboydre says:

"At seven years old, my daughter, like most other children, simply adores McDonald's Happy Meals but I simply can't justify the price so I have come up with an alternative which keeps everyone happy, most of all a mom who encourages healthy eating. I call it McMommy's!

"A McMommy's meal consists of homemade, oven baked potato wedges (20c) with a choice of one of my daughter's favorites – chicken pie, pizza or breaded chicken breast – all homemade ($1), a glass of mineral water and, of course, a toy or trinket (which I buy on sale for no more than $1 and stash away until needed).

"For a total cost of less than $2.50 my daughter gets a fun and healthy meal. She loves and looks forward to McMommy's and can't understand why other kids don't get to have such a treat!"

For more ideas to tempt the fussiest kids, you may also like to try the following recipes:

Sam's chicken soup – Luscious lunches – Page 127
Popcorn – Snazzy snacks – Page 187
Jackie's homemade burgers – Divine dinners – Page 136

Desserts

If you think your family will miss out on dessert during your Challenge week, then think again! This collection of quick and easy recipes will keep everyone happy!

Fudgy choc cookies

We all have chocolate cravings from time to time – even during a $21 Challenge week! Fortunately you only need a few pantry staples to make these indulgent cookies. Crisp on the outside; moist and velvety on the inside; who knew something so rich could be so cheap and easy to make?

2 eggs

1 cup lightly packed soft brown sugar

½ cup oil

1 tsp vanilla extract

2 cups all-purpose flour

1 tbsp baking powder

½ cup cocoa, sifted

Turn your oven on to 350F. Beat your eggs, brown sugar and oil together in a large bowl. Add vanilla, flour, baking powder and cocoa and mix well to combine. Roll teaspoonfuls of the mixture into balls. Place your balls on a greased and lined cookie sheet and flatten slightly with a fork. Bake for 12-15 minutes or until cooked through. Leave to cool on wire racks. Store in a cool place in an airtight container.

Tip: For extra chunky cookies, add half a cup of crushed nuts or cooking chocolate broken into small pieces.

CONTRIBUTED BY: RUTH KINGHORNE

Five-cup coconut and golden raisin loaf

Hugely popular with $21 Challengers, this is a wonderful cake to bake when there is 'nothing' in your cupboard. An old fashioned recipe which the contributor learned from a craft group discussion!

> *1 cup self-rising flour*
>
> *1 cup brown sugar*
>
> *1 cup milk*
>
> *1 cup coconut*
>
> *1 cup golden raisins (or you can substitute golden raisins with mixed fruit, apricots or chocolate chips with 1 tbsp cocoa)*

Mix all your ingredients together and bake in a greased and lined loaf pan at around 350F until your cake is golden, cooked through and springs back when touched, around 25 minutes. Couldn't be easier!

CONTRIBUTED BY: JAY TREACEY

Fiona's candied fruit

Turn those overripe fruit in your bowl or fridge into a yummy treat! This is a really flexible recipe for using up 3-4 pieces of fruit.

> *3-4 pieces of fruit of your choice (apples, pears, peaches, nectarines, etc. Wouldn't work with liquidy fruit like oranges)*
>
> *1 tbsp sugar (any type, brown is my favorite)*
>
> *1 tsp cinnamon*
>
> *1 tbsp oil (macadamia oil is my favorite)*

Turn your oven on to 350F. Grease a cookie sheet. Peel your fruit, chop it into wedge shapes and place it all together in a clean medium sized plastic bag. Put the sugar, cinnamon and oil in the bag with your fruit. Shake the bag vigorously until all your fruit is coated.

Pour the ingredients from the bag onto the cookie sheet. Then spread your fruit over the tray with a fork and pop it in the oven for 30 minutes or until the edges of the fruit start to brown. Absolutely delish!

Tristan's very clever popsicles

This is an all time favorite in Fiona's household! She loves it because they are made with gelatin so the popsicles don't drip sticky sweet stuff all over the house. The kids love it because it is yummy and they can make it themselves. It is cheap, fun, fast and so easy Fiona's three-year-old Tristan has claimed it as his own.

1 x 3 oz box Jell-O
1 cup hot water
1 cup cold water

You will need:

Cookie tray with raised sides
Popsicle molds
Teapot
Fork

Place your popsicle molds on the cookie tray so that any overflow is caught by the cookie tray. Make sure you have room in your freezer for the molds and the path to the freezer is clear of toys and step stools!

Pour hot water into a medium size bowl then add your Jell-O. Whisk together with a fork. When the crystals are dissolved, pour in the cold water. Stir some more. Pour mixture into molds and then freeze for 4 hours. Easy!

To see photos of Tristan making these go to:
http://www.21dollarchallenge.com/article/popsicles

Jackie's happy fruit crumble

Jackie's kids LOVE this recipe! She calls it happy fruit crumble because whenever she makes it she takes any sad looking fruit from the fruit bowl and turns them into this fantastic comforting pudding. It makes her feel happy that she's putting them to good use instead of throwing them away and it puts a smile on the whole family's faces when they dig into it!

4-5 largish pieces of fruit, peeled and sliced (apples, pears, peaches, apricots, whatever you have! If using canned fruit, drain well first)

½ cup dried fruit OR 1 cup fresh, canned or frozen berries

Juice of half a lemon (not essential but good!)

Drizzle maple syrup (optional)

1 cup flour

⅔ cup butter or margarine (or ½ cup at a push)

½ cup rolled oats

½ cup coconut

2 tbsp brown sugar

1 tsp cinnamon

Put your oven on at 350F to warm up. Place your peeled, sliced fruit in a deep baking dish. Sprinkle your dried fruit or berries over the top. Squeeze lemon juice over your fruit if using and drizzle the syrup over the top. If you don't have lemon juice or syrup, sprinkle a little extra brown sugar over the top instead. Put your oats, flour, coconut, brown sugar and cinnamon into a large bowl. Add the butter and combine all together by running the ingredients through your fingers until well mixed and crumbly (you can of course use a food processor if you don't mind the extra dishes). Scatter your crumble mixture over the fruit and bake in the oven for 50 minutes. Delicious on its own or served with ice cream, cream, custard and even milk!

Milky Way surprise slice

What's the surprise? There are no Milky Ways in this recipe! This clever recipe was dreamed up by Simple Savings member Nova Dunworth. She wanted to make a Milky Way slice – the only problem was, she didn't have any Milky Way bars. However, she wasn't about to let that stop her! This ingenious recipe tastes as good as the real thing and will use up your Rice Krispies and condensed milk in the pantry. Perfect!

1 can condensed milk

1 tbsp honey

1 tbsp corn syrup

½ stick butter

3 tsp cocoa

2½-3½ cups Rice Krispies (any brand will do)

3 tbsp butter (for topping)

7 oz dark or milk chocolate, whatever you have

Melt your condensed milk, honey, syrup and butter in a saucepan over a medium heat. Stir constantly for 10-15 minutes until it turns a caramel color. Stirring constantly will stop your mixture from burning.

Add the cocoa to your caramel and mix well. Leave to cool for 10-15 minutes. Stir in your Rice Krispies, trying not to break them too much. Things get pretty sticky at this point but the mixture will firm up on chilling. The amount you add depends on how chewy you like it – the more Rice Krispies you have the firmer the slice will be.

Press into a greased and lined slice tray and chill. When cold, make your topping by melting the chocolate with the three tablespoons of butter. Spread it on top of your Rice Krispies mixture and refrigerate until required.

CONTRIBUTED BY: NOVA DUNWORTH

Golden raisin muffins

This recipe takes a little preparation beforehand but the results are well worth it. Allow an hour or so to cook and cool your fruit first, then you can proceed with the rest of the recipe.

1½ cups golden raisins

1½ cups water

½ cup butter

½ cup sugar

1 egg

1 tsp vanilla extract

1½ cups self-rising flour

Put your golden raisins, water, butter and sugar into a saucepan and bring to the boil. Simmer for 2 minutes, remove from the heat and leave to cool for at least an hour.

Once your fruit has cooled, turn your oven on to 400F. Transfer the saucepan mixture into a large bowl. Add the egg, vanilla and flour and give it a good stir. Spoon the mixture into greased muffin pans and cook at 400F for 15 minutes. Just delicious!

CONTRIBUTED BY: HELEN T.

Quick apple and cinnamon dessert

All you need are a few basic ingredients to turn a single apple into this comforting, filling dessert. One of the fastest puddings we know, this recipe comes from Jackie's mom!

> 2 tbsp honey
>
> 1 tbsp corn syrup (or 2 if you like it a little sweeter)
>
> 1 apple
>
> 1 cup self-rising flour
>
> ½ cup butter or margarine, melted
>
> ½ cup sugar
>
> 6 tbsp milk
>
> ½ tsp baking powder
>
> ½ tsp cinnamon

Stir your honey and corn syrup in the bottom of a medium sized microwave-proof bowl. Peel and slice your apple and place in the bottom of the bowl (and around the sides if you need to). Mix all other ingredients together and pour over your apple. Microwave on high for 6 minutes, then stand for 5 minutes. Serve with custard, whipped cream or ice cream. Easy as that!

> For more decadent treats check out these recipes too!
>
> Condensed milk ice cream – Bonus meals – Page 207
> No-egg cookies – Bonus meals – Page 221
> Flummery – Bonus meals – Page 223
> Rich chocolate sauce – Bonus meals – Page 212

Snazzy snacks

Some of us snack, some don't. Jackie never snacks, but the rest of her family do! To keep them happy during a $21 Challenge week she bakes her heart out. She'll spend a whole morning in the kitchen and make enough goodies to fill the cookie jar and freezer and see her family through the week.

Have plenty of 'instant food' for your Challenge

It doesn't matter how you plan your snacks for your Challenge week, as long as you do it! Your week will be easier if there is plenty to eat without having to give in to the kids or hubby mid-week and slope off to the store. These recipes show you how to keep everyone happy with next to no effort or ingredients. When planning your snacks, make sure you:

1. Always have food ready and waiting.

When guys and kids open the fridge or pantry, they want something to eat, and they want it right NOW! They don't want to fluff about finding food or throwing together a meal – they want something ready to throw straight down the hatch, whether it be a muffin, scone or piece of fruit.

2. Tell them where it is so they can FIND it!

Don't laugh... in our experience most guys and teenagers cannot see what is in front of their noses! Making sure they know where everything is will really help avoid the dreaded 'There's nothing to eat!' scenario.
An easy way to make sure everyone has access to fast, good food when they want it is to keep a list of snacks on hand stuck to the fridge. This works well for the whole family, even young kids. Food is available at a glance; all they have to do is check the list and grab whatever they feel like from the freezer or pantry.

Keeping the family supplied with snacks does not mean you have to be chained to the kitchen! You can whip up a week's worth of snacks in no time using these quick and tasty recipes. It's quicker than going to the store and better still, they can make many of the recipes themselves!

Miss Jacqueline's softer than soft sponge

Fiona's daughter, Miss Jacqueline has been making this gluten-free, dairy-free, preservative-free sponge cake since she was four years old. You can watch her demonstrating the recipe on YouTube.

The keys to making a successful sponge is to make sure your mixing bowl is clean and dry and you have everything ready before you crack the first egg.

> *4 eggs, separated*
>
> *1 tsp cream of tartar*
>
> *½ tsp baking soda*
>
> *1 cup cornstarch*
>
> *¾ cup superfine sugar*
>
> *Dash of vanilla extract*

Pre-heat your oven to 350F and line your cake pan with greaseproof paper. TWICE sift your tartar, baking soda and cornstarch together.

Separate your eggs. Place egg whites in a clean bowl and beat them on high till they are light and fluffy. Keep your beaters on high while you pour in your superfine sugar. Reduce speed to medium, add vanilla and then egg yolks one at a time. Sift dry ingredients into your bowl and fold in gently with an egg whisk. Pour mixture into cake pan and bake for 20 minutes or until it smells cooked.

A houseful of cookies

Where can you get over 120 delicious cookies for just $4? With this fantastic bulk recipe! Simple Savings members have been making these cookies for years thanks to member Kristy Frahm. Make up the basic cookie recipe below and enjoy them plain or adapt them to use up all sorts of odds and ends from your pantry – chocolate chips, nuts, cinnamon, the options are endless. The raw mixture can also be frozen in balls; just thaw slightly before baking and pull out when needed during your $21 Challenge week!

Basic cookie mixture:

1 cup sugar

1 lb margarine

1 can condensed milk

5 cups self-rising flour

Turn your oven on to 350F and grease a large cookie sheet. Put your margarine and sugar together in a large bowl and beat until pale and creamy. Add your condensed milk and flour to the bowl and mix together well. You can add any of your own extra ingredients too at this point, if using. Stir until well combined.

Roll your mixture into teaspoon-sized balls and place on your greased cookie sheet. Press down gently on the cookies with a fork to flatten slightly. Bake in the oven for 10-15 minutes until golden brown.

CONTRIBUTED BY: KRISTY FRAHM

That's all there is to it. We challenge you to find a more economical recipe anywhere, and its flexibility is unmatched!

Over the years, Simple Savings members have come up with a staggering 107 different ways to adapt these basic cookies! While unfortunately we can't include them all in this book, here are 15 successful combinations to get your brain ticking. See how many you can come up with using bits and pieces from your own pantry!

Try adding any of the following to your basic mix:

1. M&M's

2. Coconut

3. Chocolate malted milk powder and choc chips

4. A squeeze of orange juice and some finely grated zest

5. Nutmeg, cinnamon and ginger

6. Honey and rolled oats

7. Dried fruit

8. Rice Krispies

9. Ground almonds

10. Peanut butter

11. Rocky road – peanuts, marshmallows and choc chips

12. Muesli

13. Vanilla extract

14. Crushed cornflakes

15. Choc-mint – cocoa and peppermint extract

For the full list of 107 variations to this recipe, as dreamed up by Simple Savings members, go to:

www.21dollarchallenge.com/recipes

Bread maker loaf for hungry teens

How many of us have bread makers sitting unused in the cupboard? Many people try them out only to find the novelty wears off after the first few loaves. After all that time and effort, the family eats the whole thing in five minutes flat and it's easier to just go and buy a loaf than constantly having to churn out more. We know, we've been there! However, if you have hungry teenagers in your house, go and dust your bread maker off! You can save a bundle on expensive snacks and junk food by using it to whip up an economical afternoon snack to fill the emptiest tummies.

Teenage boys in particular have hollow legs. One of the best tricks we know is to put the bread maker on in the morning so it is set to finish when the boys get home from school. The smell draws them in and they consume the entire fifty cent loaf before looking for anything else in the kitchen. It stops them from eating entire bags of cookies or chips or a week's worth of baking the moment they walk through the door. When you compare the cost of a homemade loaf of bread to those cookies or chips, it's obviously far more economical, not to mention healthier.
The kids will think you're a legend too!

Flavored bread suggestions: For a tasty alternative that will also use up some bits and pieces from your kitchen inventory, try adding the following to your usual bread mix:

> ¾ cup cooked mashed pumpkin, or
>
> ½ sautéed onion, or
>
> ⅓ cup sun-dried tomatoes, or
>
> ¼ cup of chopped bacon, or
>
> ½ cup grated cheese, or
>
> 4 tbsp pesto

Cream of anything cup-a-soup

Simple Savings member Paula Nowicki is an amazing lady. She can make just about anything from scratch – and we mean anything! If you can buy it, she can make it. Her recipe for homemade cup-a-soup can turn all sorts of leftover bits and pieces into a delicious snack.

To make the creamy soup base, combine the following in a screw-top jar and shake. This mix will last for 12 months.

4 cups powdered milk

1½ cups cornstarch

½ cup chicken booster (stock powder)

4 tsp dried onion flakes

2 tsp dried thyme

2 tsp dried basil

1 tsp pepper

To make your cup-a-soup, put a third of a cup of the mix into a mug and top up with hot water.

To make your soup taste extra special you can add a tablespoon or two of the following to your mug:
Finely sliced mushrooms and celery • chopped asparagus • cooked diced potato and ham • cooked shredded chicken and small pieces of broccoli • small pieces of cooked meat • cooked shrimps.

This soup recipe can also be used as a casserole base in place of a can of creamed soup.

CONTRIBUTED BY: PAULA NOWICKI

Dips

Dips are a fantastic snack to fall back on during Challenge week. But many people don't realize dips don't have to come out of a tub. You can make your own in a matter of seconds! All you need is something creamy, such as mayo or sour cream and goodies for flavor, such as sun-dried tomatoes, fresh herbs and seasoning. Then you throw all the ingredients into the blender, turn it on, add some water (or oil if it is too thick). And, taadaa! You have dip. If you don't have a blender, make your dip by chopping any chunky ingredients finely, then throw everything in a bowl and mash it together with a fork. Both methods work well and are very simple. The best bit is, you can make them out of almost anything. Here is a list of the dip recipes in this book. Read through them and give them a go if you have the ingredients. If not, make up a new dip recipe with the food you already have. It will be an exciting new taste sensation!

Easy chocolate slice

This recipe is a brilliant way to use up that bag of plain cookies that nobody liked in the pantry! Kids love it because they can make it themselves; all it takes is four easy steps.

1 bag plain cookies, fresh or stale

7 oz butter

2 tbsp sugar

2 tbsp cocoa

1 egg

7 oz cooking chocolate for melting

Crush your bag of cookies by putting them in a plastic bag, wrapping in a tea towel and beating with fists or a rolling pin until they resemble crumbs (if you can get the kids to help with this part, so much the better!). Pour your crumbs into a large mixing bowl.

Melt your butter for 30 seconds or so until melted. Add the sugar and cocoa to the butter and mix well. Add the egg and stir well again.

Add your butter mixture to the crushed cookies and stir through until well combined. Pour into a greased cookie tray and press your cookie mixture firmly into the pan. Refrigerate for 30 minutes.

Melt the cooking chocolate and spread over the top. Leave long enough for the chocolate to harden before eating. YUM!

CONTRIBUTED BY: ANGELA HANSEN

Fruity yogurt muffins

This recipe is a delicious way to use up all that yogurt sitting in your fridge. This is another popular choice among $21 Challengers as you can adapt this recipe to suit whatever you have on hand.

½ cup margarine

½ cup sugar

2 eggs

¾ cup fruit yogurt

3 oz milk (or more if needed)

6 oz fresh strawberries, chopped (fresh, frozen or canned fruit)

1 lemon, juice and rind

2½ cups self-rising flour

Heat up the oven to 350F and line or grease your muffin pans. Cream your margarine and sugar together until fluffy, then beat in your eggs, yogurt and milk. Fold in your chopped fruit, lemon juice and rind, then gently fold in the flour.

Spoon your mixture into your muffin tray and bake for about 20 minutes, or longer if you use frozen fruit.

Kerrie says: I left out the milk and just used yogurt (because I was trying to use it up). I just added a squirt of lemon juice rather than the juice of a whole lemon and rind, and I used apple and peaches in place of the strawberries. They're incredibly moist!

CONTRIBUTED BY: KERRIE PTOLEMY

Liam's quick baked potatoes

Jackie's son Liam is a great example of how well the snack list works. It shows him exactly where all the ready-made food is, as well as suggestions of quick things he can make for himself. One of his favorite snacks is microwaved 'baked potatoes'. This warm and filling snack takes just five minutes. Perfect for hungry football-playing teenagers!

Choose a nice big potato and scrub the outside until clean. Pat dry and put in a microwave suitable bowl. Pierce the skin a few times with a fork. Brush your potato with a little oil and sprinkle with a pinch of salt.

Cook on high for 5 minutes (based on a 1200 watt microwave). Test for 'done-ness' by sticking your fork in the middle of your potato, if it still feels crunchy you need to zap it for another 30-60 seconds.

Cut your potato in half and make a few cuts in each half. Spread a little butter across each half, allowing it to melt and run into the cuts. Sprinkle with grated cheese and pop back in your microwave for 20 seconds to melt the cheese.

Enjoy steaming hot. Yum! Accompany with salad and/or green vegetables for a more substantial meal.

Don't forget to share YOUR
$21 Challenge snack ideas with us!
You could win a free Simple Savings membership! Go to:

www.21dollarchallenge.com/competition

Coconut and honey granola bars

Homemade granola bars are SO much cheaper than bought ones. This recipe makes over two pounds of yummy granola bars and costs around $4.80, which works out at around 16c per bar. Compare that figure to the price of store-bought bars (currently 80c for top brands and 39c for generic brands – PER BAR), and you can see this recipe saves you a fortune! Better still, you know exactly what's in them!

1½ cups toasted muesli (any type or make your own - see page 235)

2½ cups Rice Krispies (any brand will do)

½ cup coconut

¼ cup crushed nuts

½ cup butter

½ cup honey

½ cup peanut butter

½ cup raw sugar

½ cup choc chips (optional)

Grease and line a shallow cookie tray (we recommend a 11in x 14in tray, which makes 30 standard granola bars). Mix your muesli, Rice Krispies, coconut and nuts together in a bowl. Put your butter, honey, peanut butter and sugar into a small saucepan and stir over a low heat until melted. Bring to the boil, then reduce heat and simmer without stirring for 5 minutes. Pour melted ingredients into the bowl with your dry ingredients and stir well. Leave to cool for 20 minutes or until it reaches room temperature. Add choc chips and mix well. Spread mixture into the tray and pack in tightly, smoothing with a knife or spatula. Pop in the fridge until firm. Slice and serve. These bars will keep in the fridge for three weeks – if they last that long!

CONTRIBUTED BY: SARA DIAS

ANZAC biscuits

ANZAC biscuits are a classic Australian cookie. In the First World War Australian and New Zealand women supported their troops by sending them these nutritious, delicious, long lasting cookies. Since then they have become an Aussie and Kiwi tradition.

1 cup rolled oats

1 cup all-purpose flour

1 cup sugar

1 cup finely shredded coconut

1 stick butter

2 tbsp golden syrup (OR 1 tbsp honey + 1 tbsp corn syrup)

½ tsp baking soda

1 tbsp boiling water

Preheat your oven to 320F and lightly grease two cookie trays. Mix your oats, sifted flour, sugar and coconut in a large bowl. Then combine your butter and syrup in a small pan and stir over a gentle heat. Mix your baking soda and water in a cup and then add it to your melted butter mixture. Pour your mixture onto your dry ingredients and stir through. Take teaspoonfuls of mixture and place on your cookie sheets; allow room for spreading. Cook for 20 minutes. Loosen your cookies while they are still warm and then let the cookies cool on trays to crisp them up. Makes about 30 cookies.

NOTE: ANZAC stands for the Australian and New Zealand Army Corps. It was the nickname given to our troops in World War One. Out of respect to the ANZACs it is important ANZAC biscuits are always called ANZAC **biscuits**. They are never ANZAC cookies. Golden syrup is a traditional Austalian ingredient. It is a very light treacle. If you can find it, buy some. It is so yummy!

Vanilla pikelets

Pikelets are delicious hot or cold. Enjoy them for a mid-morning treat, as an after school snack or wrapped up in lunchboxes. Show us the child who doesn't like them! This recipe makes 30.

1½ cups all-purpose flour

1 tsp baking soda

2 tsp cream of tartar

2 tbsp sugar

2 eggs

1 tsp vanilla extract

Milk to mix

1 tbsp butter, melted

Sift your dry ingredients together in a large bowl. Make a well in the center and drop in your (unbeaten) eggs and vanilla. Add milk slowly, stirring constantly until you have added enough to make a smooth batter. Melt the butter and add to your mixture, stirring just enough to combine. Lightly grease a large frypan with a little oil or butter and turn the heat to medium. When your butter is sizzling, drop tablespoons of mixture into the pan. When bubbles appear, turn over and cook the other side until golden. If your first efforts are a little 'well done', don't worry! Just reduce the heat. These can also be cooked in a sandwich press! Close the lid and cook for a minute – no turning or over oiling!

Popcorn

Kids love making and eating their own fresh popcorn! You can buy popcorn ready-made but making your own is 10 times cheaper and so much more fun!

If you don't have a popcorn machine you can cook the kernels on your stove top – just make sure you use a pan with a lid! To make a good sized bowl, heat three tablespoons of oil in a large saucepan on a medium heat. Once the oil is hot, add five tablespoons of popcorn kernels and put the lid on, quick! Give the pan a shake from time to time to prevent any sticking to the bottom or burning. Once the popping has stopped, remove from the heat, lift up the lid carefully and take a peek to ensure they have all finished.

Super speedy scones

This tasty scone recipe is quick and easy! The scones are perfect for filling lunchboxes or as an afternoon treat during $21 Challenge week.

2 cups self-rising flour
2 tbsp (heaped) butter or margarine
Pinch salt
1 cup milk

Sift flour and salt in a bowl. Using your fingers, rub in the butter until the mixture resembles breadcrumbs. Add enough milk to make a soft dough, roll out on a floured board or counter top and cut into scones. Place on a lightly greased tray and bake at 350F for 10-12 minutes.

CONTRIBUTED BY: JENNIFER WALL

Yogurt pots

Many households buy large tubs of yogurt, only to find it regularly goes to waste. More often than not, the problem is not the yogurt but the size of the tub! When looking for a quick snack, family members don't see large tubs. They will only think to grab the yogurt if you put it in small tubs with pretty stickers and place it somewhere obvious in your fridge. If this is what you have to do to make sure all your yogurt is used up in your $21 Challenge, then go for it! Divide your large tub of yogurt into smaller containers and cover. By all means decorate the pots to make them look appealing to younger children. The yogurt will 'jump out' of the fridge at them and make them want to eat it.

You can save even more on bought yogurt for kids by making your own using the recipe on page 114 and dividing it up this way.

For more sensational snack ideas, check out these recipes too!

Jackie's gourmet pies – Luscious lunches – Page 122
Fruity yogurt muffins – Snazzy snacks – Page 182
Wheat germ and banana snacks – Bonus meals – Page 253

Part 6
Bonus meals –
turning clutter into cuisine!

"Having just done my first $21 Challenge, the hardest thing for me was trying to work out what to do with all the stuff I had – I seemed to only have half the ingredients of any meal I thought of to make. This was a hard mindset to break (running to the store or trying to find a recipe which used all the ingredients I already had) until I worked out the obvious for myself. I COULD be creative with dinner and I COULD improvize with alternatives. It isn't about starting with a recipe and then trying to find the ingredients, it's about starting with the ingredients and then dreaming up the recipe!"

BELLA KNIGHT

Make meals from mysterious ingredients

Thanks to the wonders of menu planning and the recipes in this book, you should now have a pretty good idea how you can use up all sorts of things in your fridge, pantry and freezer. But what about all the stuff in your bonus meals box? Have you thought of any ways to use up those random ingredients and turn them into meals yet?

Your bonus meals box no doubt still contains quite a few things that you have absolutely no idea what to do with. Things you bought which seemed like a really good idea at the time but once you confined them to your pantry, they never made it back out. You have already invested money in these items so it's crazy not to use them up. Fortunately, when it comes to using things up we are experts!

With the help of our members, we came up with this list of common items found in many bonus meals boxes. See how many items from your own box you can match up and make part of your $21 Challenge. Who knows, they may become family favorites and end up on your list of pantry regulars instead!

You will see we have included recipes where appropriate with some items but mainly this section is made up of tips to get your brain going. We're not giving you all the answers here, merely a springboard to help you learn new skills. Once you work out what you CAN do with an ingredient from your bonus meals box, it is up to you to go and find an appropriate recipe to make it. We highly recommend a Google search!

This chapter is in alphabetical order. To help you turn to the page you need, without having to flick through everything, we have included a simple index to make your life easier.

Bonus ingredient index

Artichokes

Not simply a big thistle, artichokes are high in vitamin A and C, as well as calcium and iron. However, marinated artichokes are one of those foods that people tend to buy and then allow to sit inside the fridge door for months because they have no idea what they're supposed to do with them. This is a real shame because they can be used to make some delicious meals!

Dip

Blend marinated artichokes with Parmesan, olive oil and chives for a fantastic dip. Drain a jar of marinated artichokes, then chop and blend. Pour in one third of a cup of olive oil with blender running. Then mix in finely chopped chives and two thirds of a cup of Parmesan or grated cheese. Season to taste. Perfect with pita bread chips, Turkish bread or crackers.

Frittata

Artichokes are perfect in quiche or frittata. Simply chop finely and sauté with your other favorite vegetables when making your usual recipe.

Pizza

For a delicious lunch or light meal spread tomato paste, artichokes and any cooked meat or veggies you like on a pizza crust. Sprinkle with grated cheese and pop it in the oven. If you don't have any pizza crusts, just use toast and pop it under the grill. Simple, lazy and so yummy!

Salads

Artichokes are a refreshing addition to all kinds of salads. They are especially delicious in potato salad, caesar salad and green salad.

Beets (canned)

Most of us have a can of beets taking up room in the pantry. Don't leave it sitting there! Open it up and unleash loads of color and flavor. Beets are one of the sweetest vegetables available, naturally containing around 8% sugar. Here's how you can make the most of your can, as well as serving it the traditional way; cold with roast meat of course!

Baked potatoes

Beets taste fantastic in a baked potato! Sauté a little diced onion and bacon in a frypan and add some chopped canned beets to the pan. Heat gently until everything is warmed through, then serve over a baked potato with a dollop of sour cream.

Burgers

Next time you enjoy homemade burgers at home, pop some sliced beets in the bun to add color and zing to the usual lettuce and tomato combo.

Beetiful dip

Beet dip is so bright and cheery! Simply blend one can of drained beets with a block of cream cheese in the food processor. Enjoy with veggie sticks, pita bread chips or your favorite crackers.

Quick pasta

A really easy way to use up canned beets is to turn them into a tasty pasta. Just drain your beets and cut them into thin strips. Search your fridge for more goodies such as parsley, tomatoes or mushrooms and slice these up too. Add to the beets along with a handful of grated cheese. Throw on top of steaming hot cooked pasta and stir through.

Salad

So many things taste delicious combined with beets. Grated carrot, parsley, lettuce, baby spinach, rocket leaves, sweet potato, tomato, chickpeas, cheddar, feta, even orange – the list goes on. Add it to coleslaw for extra color and bite. This is one vegetable you can be really creative with and enjoy almost guaranteed success. Give it a go and see what yummy salad recipes you can invent in your Challenge week!

Sandwich

Cheese and beets go together beautifully in a salad, so why not combine them in a sandwich? To stop the bread from going soggy, dry the beets on paper towels before adding it to your sandwich. As a variation, make a tasty sandwich spread by blending beets with mayonnaise.

Cabbage

Cabbage is often found in people's 'bonus meal' lists. You buy a huge cabbage, hack a bit off it and then never seem quite able to use up the rest! However, its nutritional benefits are huge so don't let those leaves go to waste! Here are some great ideas:

Asian salad

Finely chop half a cabbage and two sticks of celery. Place in a large bowl with two thinly sliced carrots. Mix well together and stir through a handful of finely chopped toasted almonds or crispy noodles if you have them. To make the dressing, combine half a cup of olive oil, half a cup of brown sugar, one teaspoon of vinegar and one teaspoon of soy sauce.

Coleslaw

For a basic, yummy coleslaw simply mix together one cup of finely chopped cabbage with one cup of grated carrot in a bowl. Stir through a quarter to half a cup of mayonnaise or caesar dressing to taste.

Shepherd's pie

Add a touch of variety to your usual shepherd's pie. Finely chop or blend one to two cups of cabbage and add to the ground beef while cooking.

Savory ground beef

To make ground beef go further add one to two cups of finely chopped cabbage to your usual ground beef. If chopping, dice it up as small as you can. Simply add to your ground beef mixture while cooking.

Carrot

Carrots have far more uses than just helping you see better in the dark! They are an excellent source of antioxidant compounds, which help protect against cardiovascular disease and cancer. Enjoy them any way you can – try these suggestions for starters!

Carrot soup

You can make a super easy and filling carrot soup in next to no time. Simply fry one chopped onion in a little oil. Add a handful of peeled, chopped carrots and a few cups of vegetable stock, salt and pepper. Bring to the boil and simmer 20-25 minutes until the carrots are tender. Pour your soup in a blender, whiz until smooth and you're done!

Carrot sticks with dip

Peel and cut carrot into thin sticks. Serve with dip – a tub of cream cheese mixed with sweet chili sauce or onion soup mix.

Coleslaw

Carrot is a bright and tasty addition to any coleslaw. See the recipe on page 196 for details.

Hidden in ground beef

Add bulk and nutrition to your ground beef with finely grated or pureed carrot. Stir in the carrot after you have browned your ground beef and then cook as normal. Even the fussiest eaters won't complain!

In stir-fries

Carrot adds crunch, color and nutrition to stir-fries. Throw them in as circular slices, thin strips; whatever you like!

Potato bake

Carrots give a bright splash of color to any potato bake. Make your bake as usual with layers of thinly sliced potatoes, onion soup mix, grated cheese and cream. Just add an extra layer of grated carrot!

Rice paper rolls

Slice carrots into thin julienne strips. Use in rice paper rolls with vermicelli, julienned cucumber and leftover chicken breast. Serve with a sweet chili or teriyaki dipping sauce.

Cauliflower

Usually served smothered in cheese sauce, the humble cauliflower has many nutritional benefits. Low in fat, high in vitamin C and proven to reduce the risk of cancer, it's far too good to leave turning brown in the back of the fridge! Get creative with your cauli and try some of these yummy suggestions instead.

Curries

Cauliflower is especially good in your curries. Chop into small florets and add during the cooking process with your other veggies.

Mashed potatoes

To give a nutritious boost to everyday mashed spuds, cook your cauliflower in boiling water until tender. Then puree and add to cooked, mashed potatoes for a lovely creamy texture and taste.

Salad

Try this creamy cauliflower salad for a change. Chop half a cauliflower into small florets and cook until just tender. Drain and cool. Once cold, stir through a cup of coleslaw dressing or mayonnaise. To finish, toast a quarter of a cup of sesame seeds on a tray in the oven for a few minutes until golden brown. Cool then scatter over cauliflower. Serve chilled.

Soup

Cauliflower makes a delicious, filling soup. Fry one finely chopped onion in a little oil for a few minutes until soft. Add three cups of chicken stock, one peeled, chopped potato and one whole large cauliflower, chopped into florets. Bring to the boil, reduce heat and simmer for 25 minutes until the vegetables are really tender. Process until smooth in a blender and add salt and pepper to taste.

Stir-fries

Cauliflower makes a fresh tasting, crunchy addition to any stir-fry. Simply chop into small florets and add to your wok or pan.

Veggie dippers

With their handy shape and subtle flavor, raw cauliflower florets make wonderful crudite for dunking in dips and sauces. Try them with just about anything, they all taste great!

Chickpeas

Crunchy, delicious and full of protein, chickpeas are fantastic fillers in all sorts of dishes. Also known as garbanzo beans, chickpeas are tasty in stir-fries, great in soups, superb in stews and make delicious dips. They'll even bulk out your bolognaise! Note: these recipes and suggestions are all for cooked or canned chickpeas. If you are using dried, you will need to soak and cook them first.

Curries

Chickpeas are a brilliant addition to any curry, particularly vegetarian recipes and butter chicken. Simply throw them in when making your favorite recipe and enjoy the difference.

Salads

With their crunchy texture and nutty flavor, chickpeas are a refreshing addition to many salads, particularly green salads.

Snacks

Chickpeas make a super speedy and yummy snack! Just sprinkle your drained chickpeas with your favorite herbs and spices. Then lightly pan fry them.

Hummus

Fiona used to think hummus was one of those magical foods that no one actually made, it just appeared in tubs in the supermarket. She was stunned when she first found out that she could make it herself at home. Since, then she has become a hummus and dip queen. Here is her favorite hummus recipe.

1 x 14 oz can chickpeas, drained and rinsed

2 cloves garlic, finely chopped

4 tbsp tahini (sesame seed puree)

3 tbsp vinegar

¼ cup olive oil

½ tsp salt

Pinch of paprika

Little bit of hot water

Puree all the ingredients in your blender. Add some extra hot water so the dip blends easily. It is OK if your hummus is a bit runny. It will thicken after you have finished making it.

Soups and stews

To make your meat dishes go further, as well as providing extra flavor and nutrition, think chickpeas! You can pop them in all sorts of soups, casseroles and stews for a Middle Eastern touch and they even work well in family favorites such as spaghetti bolognaise and chili con carne.

Chutney and relish

Sweet, spicy and oh-so-versatile, most of us have a jar of chutney or relish lurking in the fridge. Here are a few ideas!

Curry

Chutney and curry make the perfect pair. Add a tablespoon or two of chutney or relish to curried sausages for a match made in heaven.

Dip

Whip up this yummy dip in a flash! Mix a few tablespoons of chutney or relish with a tub of cream cheese. Serve with crackers or veggie sticks.

Marinade

Chutney and relish are quite acidic so are perfect for tenderizing meat. Brush on top of steak, chops or meat skewers before cooking and everyone will marvel at your tantalizingly tender meat!

Sandwiches

The simple sandwich springs to life with a spoonful of chutney or relish. Try with either cheese, ham or beef, or almost anything that will go with ketchup. Toasted sandwiches are equally great.

Sauce

For a deliciously different sauce, add some chutney or relish to plain white sauce just before serving. Stir in a tablespoon at first, then add more until you get the flavor just right.

Coconut

Finely shredded coconut is another one of those items that people always seem to have a half-used bag of taking up space in the pantry. Put it to good use instead with some of these easy suggestions!

Crumb mix

Coconut makes an awesome crumb coating for meat! Simply coat your chosen meat in flour, followed by beaten egg, then roll in coconut to cover before gently pan frying.

Crumble topping

Add a quarter to half a cup to your usual crumble topping recipe for an extra tasty dessert.

Macaroons

An old fashioned favorite. All you need is coconut, egg and sugar to make these tasty cookies. You can find this classic recipe in cook books everywhere!

Snowdrops

The whole family will love these yummy treats! So easy to make, see page 206 for the recipe.

Coconut milk

Coconut milk is used in countless dishes all over the world – so how come so many of us still don't really know what to do with it? If you have some coconut milk sitting in your pantry or fridge, now is the time to use it up!

Coconut mash

Next time you serve up mashed spuds, surprise the family with a different variation by using coconut milk instead.

Freeze it

Powdered coconut milk makes a great alternative to canned coconut milk. However, you can always freeze leftover canned coconut milk in an airtight container or plastic bag and use it next time.

Oatmeal

There is a fantastic recipe using a can of coconut milk to make Tahitian oatmeal on page 113. It is decadent and delicious!

Rice

You can make your rice extra special by boiling it in coconut milk. All you need to do is swap some of the water you would normally use to boil the rice with coconut milk. It tastes divine!

Coconut curry. Easy, no worry!

YUM! The smell of this decadent coconut curry cooking in your oven for an hour and a half will transform your kitchen into a tropical oasis! Serves 4.

2 tbsp curry paste – tandoori, red/green curry, balti, mild curry, whatever you have

1 can coconut milk

1 tbsp brown sugar

1 tbsp lemon or lime juice

1 tbsp fish sauce (optional)

1 lb either chicken thighs, lamb or beef

9 oz sweet potato (or potato), diced

½ bell pepper (or onion or leek), sliced

5 oz snow peas (or beans or frozen peas)

Turn your oven on to 170-350F to heat up. Combine your curry paste, coconut milk, sugar, lemon or lime juice, meat and fish sauce together in a casserole dish. Bake, covered for 1 hour, stirring after 30 minutes. Stir through your snow peas, beans, peas or spinach. Cook uncovered a further 15-20 minutes. Serve with rice, couscous, dahl or pita bread.

Vegetarian option: For a vegetarian option replace the meat with two cans of butter beans and one can of chickpeas. You can include both meat AND the legumes if you want to stretch your dish a little further.

Condensed milk

Super rich and creamy, who can resist condensed milk? As a youngster Jackie remembers her father gleefully digging into condensed milk sandwiches! For others who struggle to find ways to use up their condensed milk, here are some suggestions.

Caramel topping

You only need three ingredients to make this sweet and rich caramel filling. It's ideal for pies, tarts or straight off the spoon!

1 x 12 oz can sweetened condensed milk

2 tbsp butter, chopped

4 tbsp brown sugar

Mix all your ingredients together and zap in the microwave for 5 minutes, stopping to stir it every minute. Be warned, the caramel is very hot so don't burn your mouth when licking the spoon!

Snowdrops

This could be the easiest recipe ever! Just two ingredients make 30 to 40 snowdrops. You won't believe how delicious they are until you try them!

3 cups finely shredded coconut

1 can sweetened condensed milk

Mix ingredients in a bowl. Place small unshaped drops on to a greased ovenproof tray. Cook in moderate oven until light golden brown (approximately 10-15 minutes). Remove from oven and cool on rack.

Creamy dressing

To make a delicious, creamy dressing, put your condensed milk in a bowl together with the juice of one lemon and one tablespoon of white wine vinegar. Adjust quantities for taste and thickness and add a dash of mint sauce if liked. Perfect on potatoes!

Ice cream

This homemade ice cream is a fruity summer sensation kindly contributed by Simple Savings member Jenny Roberts.

An easy to make treat that fits into the tightest budget.

1 can of sweetened condensed milk (lite is fine)
1 pint cream
Fresh fruit: strawberries, banana, mango or whatever is in season

Put your fruit into a blender and add the condensed milk and cream. Process until the mixture is thick, pour it into a container and freeze. It will be ready the next day for pure enjoyment! Another way to enjoy it is to add a teaspoon of ground ginger and a cup of grated chocolate.

Rum balls

Rum balls are a classic favorite. They make a great gift, a tasty treat and are an easy 'bring-a-plate' solution. Best of all, they contain condensed milk! They are also a great way to use up those cookies that you bought and nobody liked. There are heaps of recipes for rum balls, have a look in your recipe books or online for one that matches what you have on hand.

Corn

You can make heaps of fast and tasty meals with corn! Wrap it in tortillas, munch it in salsa or slurp it up in a yummy corn chowder. Corn is another one of those ingredients which always seem to accumulate in large numbers in people's pantries. Whether it's kernels or creamed, these suggestions should help you use it up!

Baked potatoes

Sweet corn makes a yummy filling in baked potatoes. Try combining a few tablespoons of corn with 4 ounces of tuna and a couple of teaspoons of mayonnaise. Pile on the top of steaming potatoes and dig in!

Shepherd's pie

Add drained corn kernels to your usual shepherd's pie or savory ground beef recipe for extra color and taste.

Creamed corn fritters

Jackie's husband Noel has been making these for the family forever! In the past he has adapted this basic recipe to throw in anything from finely chopped or grated vegetables to a can of drained salmon. Delicious for lunches, snacks or even as part of a main meal.

1 x 14 oz can creamed corn

1 cup all-purpose flour

1 egg

1 tsp baking powder

Salt and pepper

Put flour and baking powder into a bowl, along with a good pinch of salt and a sprinkle of pepper. Add the egg and stir, then add creamed corn. Mix everything together well. Put enough oil in a frypan to cover the bottom and put over a medium heat. Once oil is hot, drop nice big spoonfuls of mixture into the pan. Keep an eye on them as they cook. Once you can see they are golden and set underneath, flip them over carefully and finish the other side. Drain on a paper towel and keep warm until all your fritters are ready to serve.

Coriander and sweet corn soup

Sweet corn tastes and looks terrific in soups! This recipe from member Judith Long cleverly uses both kernels AND creamed corn so it's twice as easy to use them up!

1 x 14 oz can creamed corn

1 x 14 oz can corn kernels

1 chopped onion

1 tsp chicken stock powder

1 tsp ground coriander

¼ tsp chili powder

1 x 14 oz can chopped tomatoes

1½ cups tomato puree (or you can puree a can of tomatoes)

2 tsp parsley if you have it

Put chopped onion in a saucepan over medium heat with stock powder, coriander and a little juice from your can of tomatoes. Cook, stirring for a few minutes until the onion has softened. Add remaining ingredients, bring to the boil and simmer gently until heated through.

Cornflakes

Cornflakes are too good to eat only at breakfast time! Use cornflakes in these recipes and you can enjoy your favorite cereal all day long.

Breakfast muffins

For breakfast on the run, grab a healthy muffin! Add half a cup of cornflakes to your regular muffin mix for an enjoyable breakfast treat, full of texture and taste.

Cookies

Turn basic cookies into an extra crunchy treat by adding half a cup of cornflakes to your usual cookie recipe.

Crispy coating

The simple schnitzel gets a makeover with a new coat! Jazz up your schnitzel or chicken pieces by coating them with crushed cornflakes.

Tasty toppings

Crushed cornflakes make a brilliant topping on pasta bakes! Sprinkle with cheese and bake as usual until irresistibly golden. Simple as that!

Couscous

Rice may be nice, but couscous makes for a refreshing change. It's a low-fat source of complex carbohydrates which can be eaten hot or cold and used in many recipes. Better still, it's SO quick to cook!

Breakfast

Simple Savings members love couscous for breakfast! Claire cooks hers up with milk, sugar and cinnamon. Kim cooks hers and then adds ricotta cheese, a sprinkle of cinnamon and some chopped fruit. Give it a go!

Instant couscous

For a super speedy snack put some couscous in a bowl. Pour boiling water over the grains and cover for two minutes. Serve under casseroles as you would with spuds or enjoy it by itself with a tablespoon of butter.

Pilaf

For a tasty main or side dish, toss cooked chicken, pork or beef into a bowl of cooked couscous. Add some raisins, nuts (almonds or cashews are ideal), fr½en peas and a sprinkling of spice. Heat through and serve.

Salad

For a salad with a difference prepare couscous according to the package and let cool. Add lots of fresh chopped parsley (or mint and basil if you prefer), diced shallots, red onions and more ingredients if you like. Dress with a lemon and olive oil vinaigrette. A little like tabouleh, only lighter.

Cream

How can it be that something as scrumlicious as cream always gets left at the back of the fridge to 'go bad'? Simple – most of the time we have to buy far more cream than we actually need. The recipe states a quarter of a cup, yet we have to buy a full bottle! Cream freezes really well so you can always store any leftovers in the freezer in airtight bags or container.

Gourmet scrambled eggs

Jazz up everyday scrambled eggs by substituting your usual milk for cream when whisking your eggs together before cooking.

Ice cream

Homemade ice cream is a favorite with everyone. To find out how easy it is to make this delicious treat, check out the recipe under condensed milk on page 207 in this section.

Mashed potato

Add cream to everyday mashed potatoes in place of milk for a luxurious mash everyone will love.

Rich chocolate sauce

For the best chocolate sauce EVER, melt two-thirds of a family size bar of dark chocolate with your cream, either in the microwave or on the stove top and stir. Serve over ice cream, banana split, strawberries or pudding.

Savory sauces

Add cream to your favorite pasta bake for a touch of decadence. Also perfect for pasta sauces like carbonara and alfredo. Check out the pasta with chicken, white wine and cream recipe on page 144.

Scones

For super light and fluffy scones, just add cream, either to your mixture or on top! Scour your recipe books or get online to find a recipe which suits the ingredients you have on hand.

Soups

When it comes to cream in soups and sauces you can use a little, or a lot! Cream is the basis for some wonderful soups – cream of chicken, cream of tomato, cream of mushroom, cream of celery; too many to list. Garnish soups such as pumpkin or leek and potato with a swirl of cream for a yummy taste sensation.

Whip it!

Whipped cream makes a fantastic topping in so many desserts! Use a hand whisk or electric beater to whip the cream until it forms soft peaks. Serve on top of stewed fruit, apple crumble, ice cream sundaes, warm chocolate brownies, you get the idea!

Cream cheese

Cream cheese is a great ingredient to have on hand and will last for ages in the fridge. However, it won't last forever, especially once opened, so use it up any way you can with the help of these suggestions!

Cheesecake

Who could forget the number one use for cream cheese – cheesecake! However, there are so many recipes for cheesecake we'll leave it up to you to find one you like!

Lemon and cream cheese icing

Carrot cake wouldn't be carrot cake without cream cheese icing! Smooth, creamy and delicious, you have to try it!

3 tbsp butter or margarine

¼ cup cream cheese

1 cup powdered sugar

1 tsp grated lemon rind

Put the butter and cream cheese in a bowl and beat together until smooth and free of lumps. Add the powdered sugar a little at a time, beating well each time until smooth. Add the grated lemon rind, stir until combined and spread across your cake (make sure the cake is completely cold first).

Dips

Blend one tub of cream cheese with a package of onion soup or four tablespoons of sweet chili sauce for a stunning and simple dip. Enjoy with crackers or fresh veggie sticks.

Baked spuds

Cream cheese tastes fantastic on baked spuds! Remove your baked potatoes hot from the oven and cut in half. Make a few slits in the flesh of each half. Garnish with a dollop of cream cheese and allow it to melt into the flesh. Delicious!

Pasta sauce

Add a quarter of a cup of cream cheese to your favorite pasta sauce to make it taste deliciously creamy and cheesy.

Pies/pastries/crepes

Cream cheese makes an awesome filling nestled in pastry. Try mixing cream cheese with mushrooms and pine nuts and using it to fill filo or puff pastry or crepes.

Spread it

Use cream cheese as a base spread on your sandwiches, bagels or crackers instead of butter or margarine. So good!

Curry paste

Whether it's red, yellow, green or whatever, you will find half empty jars of curry paste lurking in many fridges. Put those delicious herb and spice blends to good use with some of these handy tips instead!

Casseroles

Curry paste makes an excellent flavor base for all kinds of meat dishes. If you don't have enough paste to make an actual curry, just add a dollop to your casserole and you will be surprised how much flavor it adds. You can also add a little curry paste to cooked ground meat to turn bolognaise into a more spicy nachos mix. It's so easy!

Curry dip

Try this delicious carrot dip for a spicy treat even the kids will love! Peel and grate three carrots. Finely chop one onion. Squeeze the juice from two oranges. Put your fruit and vegetables in a small saucepan with one tablespoon of curry paste. Bring to the boil over medium heat, cover and simmer for 10 minutes. Process the mixture in a blender until smooth and leave to cool. Stir in two-thirds of a cup of plain yogurt and a handful of finely shredded basil leaves. Add two tablespoons of lemon juice and a pinch of salt and pepper and stir through before serving.

Curry sauce

This easy curry sauce tastes delicious with just about anything! Put one 14 oz can of tomatoes in a blender with two teaspoons of curry paste and three quarters of a cup of cream. Whiz together until well combined. To serve, simply add cooked meat or chicken and heat everything through until piping hot.

Freeze it

Curry paste freezes well in small amounts. Try freezing leftover curry paste in ice cube trays. Once frozen, pop the cubes out and freeze in an airtight container for up to three months.

Leftovers

You can turn pretty much anything into a curry! Curries are by nature a hodgepodge of vegetables and meat, which makes them ideal for using up all sorts of leftovers. Simply adapt your favorite curry recipe to include your leftovers.

Side dish

This fruity side dish is the perfect accompaniment to any curry. Fry one teaspoon of curry paste in a small pan with a sliced banana and a few tablespoons of plain yogurt. Stir well to combine and enjoy a generous dollop on the side of your main meal.

Dried fruit

If you think dried fruit is only for using in fruit cakes, think again!
Dried fruit is a great portable food for eating on the run and can
really help ensure you keep up your recommended '5+ a day'.
Adding dried fruit to your recipes is a great way to make your food
a little more nutritious. Not only are they good for your body but
they also can boost the texture and flavor. You can use dried fruit in
many recipes that call for fresh or frozen fruit. In general, just use
half as much dried fruit as you would fresh. Dig out your dried fruit
and try them in some of these suggestions!

Dried apricots

Next time you make stuffing to serve with roast meat, add some chopped
dried apricots to your usual stuffing mix. They also taste delicious in a
chicken sandwich (especially with cream cheese!). Add chopped, dried
apricots to cooked couscous or rice for extra color and flavor. Or, for
a real sweet treat, dip whole dried apricots into a bowl or pan of dark
melted chocolate. Coat to cover and leave on a flat surface for the
chocolate to harden. So good, you have to try it!

Golden raisins

Golden raisins are a natural choice for cakes, cookies and desserts, but
the warm rounded flavor also goes extremely well with savory ingredients
such as meat, fish and poultry. Add a cup of golden raisins to your next
curry or casserole and enjoy the flavor boost.

Prunes and dates

Stuff them! Take 24 dried pitted prunes and stuff with half a walnut. Mix half a cup of port with half a cup of water and soak the stuffed prunes for 30 minutes. Wrap the prunes in bacon and bake at 400F for around 10-12 minutes until the bacon is crispy.

You can stuff dates with any of the following: marzipan, whole or ground nuts, cream cheese or glace fruits like cherries or pineapple. Serve in pretty, frilly cupcakes just like fancy petit fours! Or finely chop your dates and use in puddings, cakes, breads, scones or sandwiches.

Raisins

Raisins are great with oatmeal, in cinnamon rolls, muffins, scones and just about anything else! Before adding to a recipe, plump them by microwaving them in a little water for a minute or two. You can even plump them in a little liqueur before adding them to muffins or specialty breads for extra flavor.

Other ways you can use dried fruit

- Making muesli
- added to smoothies
- made into trail mix
- use any combination of dried fruit and nuts and keep in resealable bags for a healthy snack whenever you like
- added to cereal or oatmeal
- added to plain yogurt
- added to salads
- on its own – just grab a handful and enjoy!

Drinking chocolate

Most of us have hot chocolate powder sitting unloved and unused in the pantry. Don't just save it for cold winter days! Here are some sweet suggestions to help you use it up.

Chocoholics coffee

For a really smooth and luxurious coffee, try putting a heaped teaspoon of chocolate milk powder in your coffee instead of a teaspoon of sugar. Okay, it's not the healthiest recipe we know – but it tastes so good!

Chocolate spread

Next time you have an uncontrollable chocolate craving, try this! Mash some drinking chocolate together with a little butter and vanilla extract. You can spread it on a sweet cookie, use it as icing on a cake, use as filling in a chocolate jam roll or just enjoy it straight off the spoon!

Cocoa substitute

Wherever a recipe calls for cocoa it can usually be substituted with chocolate drinking powder. The final result won't be exactly the same but there won't be too many complaints!

Instant drinking chocolate

This recipe will make seven cups of hot chocolate. Find a large, clean screw-top jar and put in two cups of full cream milk powder and half a cup of drinking chocolate. Shake the jar until both powders are well mixed.

You now have instant hot chocolate powder, ready to drink whenever you like! To serve, simply scoop three tablespoons of the powder mix into a mug, fill with hot water and enjoy. So fast and easy!

No-egg cookies

This decadent chocolate cookie recipe, which contains no eggs, is a lifesaver when you need some goodies but have no eggs in the house.

1 stick butter
¼ cup superfine sugar
1 cup self-rising flour
¼ cup drinking chocolate
Pinch of salt

Start by preheating your oven to 350F and greasing your cookie sheet. Cream the butter and sugar together until light and fluffy. Put in your flour, hot chocolate and salt. Mix all the ingredients together well. Roll your mixture into balls, place on a greased cooking sheet and flatten slightly with a fork (make sure you leave enough room between each one for it to spread a little). Bake for 10 minutes.

CONTRIBUTED BY: KIM BROOKS

Sprinkle it

Sprinkle decorating is a quick and easy way to give your baked goodies that professional touch. Put some drinking chocolate in a clean, dry salt and pepper shaker and use it to decorate cappuccinos, cakes and cookies. Tastes as good as it looks!

Eggplant

What can we say about eggplants? They are also known as aubergines, they look wonderful on the shelf all big and purple and glossy. They're also very good for you – and most of us don't have a clue what we're supposed to do with them. Don't despair! Now is your chance to experiment with some of these egg-citing solutions.

Baba ganoush

Eggplant is the main ingredient in the popular dip, baba ganoush. Making it is a lot like making hummus but instead of using chickpeas you use eggplant. To prepare the eggplant, first heat your oven to 400F. Prick your eggplant in several places with a fork, so it doesn't explode. Bake in the oven for 40 minutes. Take out of the oven and leave to cool. Scoop the eggplant out of the skin then mix with tahini, lemon juice, oil, garlic, salt and pepper as if you are making hummus (see recipe for hummus on page 201). Puree and enjoy! Baba ganoush also makes a delicious sandwich spread.

Gourmet burgers

Instead of sticking half an eggplant back in the fridge never to surface again, slice it all up and cook the lot. Once cooked you can use it in anything – curries, stir-fries and our favorite; slapped in burgers!

Roast eggplant stack

Slice your eggplant to about 1cm thick. No need to salt it before cooking. Lay the slices out on baking paper in an oven tray and brush with oil.

Cook at 350F for 10-12 minutes on each side. Stack on a plate. Accompany with sliced bell peppers, zucchini and tomato if liked for extra color and flavor.

Roasted in salads

Eggplant makes a tasty and unusual addition to warm salads. Heat the oven to 350F. Dice your eggplant into 2cm pieces and put in a shallow roasting or oven tray with a little oil. Cook in the oven for 20 minutes, remove and toss through your salad.

Veggie medley

Mix cubed, cooked eggplant with roasted red peppers, onions and garlic and drizzle balsamic vinaigrette over the top.

Evaporated milk

With its long shelf life, a can of evaporated milk is a handy thing to have in your pantry. It's also a great way to enjoy that creamy taste in cooking, without all the calories that usually go with it!

Flummery dessert

Funny name, fun to make. All you need is Jell-O and milk! Make up your Jell-O according to the directions, but only put in the one cup of hot water. Allow the Jell-O to partially set, but ensure it stays nice and wobbly – be careful not to let it get too hard and lumpy. Add 1 cup of milk and beat all the ingredients together until it is light and fluffy. Now you can leave it to set properly and enjoy!

Low-fat curry

Evaporated milk will save the day if you are a curry lover! Add to your usual curry recipe in place of cream for a luxuriously creamy, lower fat dish.

Macaroni cheese

Use evaporated milk in place of milk in your usual recipe for this traditional family favorite.

Milk

Evaporated milk is a real lifesaver when you run out of fresh milk! Simply substitute an equal amount of evaporated milk for your usual milk.

Pasta sauce

Evaporated milk makes a delicious sauce for pasta or pasta bake. Place evaporated milk in a saucepan and add a handful of grated cheese or Parmesan and a sprinkling of black pepper. Stir over gentle heat until nice and hot, then pour over your cooked pasta. You can also use evaporated milk to make the 'Lite and creamy veggie pasta' on page 146.

Scalloped potatoes

For super creamy scalloped potatoes, use evaporated milk! Turn your oven on to 350F and grease a large, shallow baking dish. Peel 4-6 decent sized potatoes and cut into thin slices. Peel and slice one onion. Layer the potatoes and onion on top of one another in the baking dish. Sprinkle with salt and pepper along the way. Dot butter or margarine over the top and pour on your can of evaporated milk. Cover and bake for one hour. Remove the cover and bake for a further 30 minutes. For extra taste try adding some finely chopped bacon when making your layers.

Four bean mix

Four bean mix is nature's super food in a can! They are an excellent source of fiber and protein, not to mention vitamins and minerals.

Baked potatoes

Four bean mix works a treat on top of hot baked potatoes with a sprinkling of grated cheese. For Mexican-style spuds, mix the beans with a good spoonful of tomato salsa and place a blob of sour cream on top.

Meat filler

Make your ground beef go twice as far! Heat a little oil in a large saucepan. Brown the ground beef all over and add a sliced onion, one 14 oz can of tomatoes and a package of onion soup. Add the drained beans and cook on low for about 20 minutes. It's magic with mashed potatoes! Great for making any ground beef dish go further – add beans to your usual recipe for extra flavor and texture. Perfect in spaghetti bolognaise or chili con carne!

Nachos

Never have nachos been so delicious – or so good for you! Simply mix your can of beans with garlic, onion, bell peppers and spices such as cumin, cardamom and chili. Pour over corn chips and enjoy!

Salads

Add four bean mix to any salad for extra color, texture and nutrition. They are particularly good in Italian-style salads, with plenty of fresh tomatoes. You can even serve the beans on their own in a small bowl; they are always a hit at barbecues served this way.

Fruit (canned)

Fiona is guilty of buying canned fruit when it is on special, then forgetting it is in the pantry. It's a bit of a shame because just one can of fruit can make all sorts of fabulous muffins and delectable desserts, just like these!

Custard

Fiona used to think that you could only make custard from custard powder. It was a bit of a shock when she discovered you can also make it from milk powder, sugar, eggs and cornstarch! Still, if you have custard powder gathering dust in your pantry, you can get rid of two things at once by serving your family canned fruit with creamy custard poured over the top for dessert.

Fruit gelatin cups

A great way to use up a large can of fruit is to make gelatin cups. Kids love 'em! This recipe makes eight yummy fruit cups. You need:

1 large can fruit of your choice (do not use pineapple as it won't set)
2 tbsp powdered gelatin
7 oz boiling water
8 small, clean containers

First, drain all the juice/syrup from your can of fruit into a bowl and put it aside. Chop the fruit into smaller pieces so it is easy for little ones to eat. Boil the kettle and pour 7 oz of hot water into a separate bowl. Add two teaspoons of powdered gelatin to the hot water and stir until it is dissolved, then add the fruit and juice. Stir it all together, then scoop into your prepared containers and pop in the fridge to set.

If you don't have any gelatin, replace the two tablespoons of gelatin with two packs of Jell-O. This version isn't as healthy, but oh boy do the kids love it!

School lunches

Canned fruit makes a great school-time snack, particularly if you have run out of fresh fruit. Just split your can or large container into several small containers and refrigerate for two or three days or a week in the freezer.

Tutti frutti muffins

Baking is a great way to use up canned fruit. Try this for 'never fail' muffins!

1 cup flour

2 tsp baking powder

½ tsp salt

½ cup sugar

½ cup milk

¼ cup butter

1 egg

Canned fruit, drained

Preheat your oven to 325F. Mix the flour, baking powder, sugar and salt in a bowl. In a separate bowl, mix the milk, butter and egg, then add your drained, canned fruit. Mix the 'wet' ingredients into the 'dry' ingredients and stir just to combine. Bake for 15-20 minutes.

Filling suggestions include: lemon, blueberry, cream cheese, peaches, apricots, apple, golden raisins and nutmeg. Don't be afraid to experiment as you can't go wrong, no matter what you use!

Gelatin

Fiona wouldn't be without gelatin in her pantry. She uses it for all sorts of things. Jackie, however, has a whole box that she doesn't know what to do with. If this sounds like you, have a go at some of these! Each brand of gelatin uses different quanitites of liquid. So follow the directions on your gelatin box for wonderful results.

Cheesecake

Use gelatin in recipes for refrigerated cheesecakes for a delicious, smooth cheesecake that won't flop!

Extra special gelatin

Turn everyday clear gelatin into something amazing by adding flowers! Nasturtiums or borage flowers look fabulous and are safe to eat.

Fruit gelatin cups

Fiona's family's favorite! See recipe on page 226.

Party cake

If you set your gelatin in a large mold you can use it as a party cake. Decorated with candies or fruit, it makes a brilliant birthday cake.
Add it to leftover cake and top with cream or yogurt for a fabulous trifle!

Lentils

These days, lentils are more hip than hippy! They have been an essential staple across the world for thousands of years so don't leave them sitting idle in your pantry! Full of iron and protein and packed with great taste, these tiny dried beans are worth their weight in gold. Lentils need no pre-soaking either, so are much faster to cook than other dried legumes. Enjoy delicious meat-free meals in 10 minutes flat!

Curries

Lentils are a staple ingredient in India and are a tasty addition to any curry recipe you have on your book shelf. Simply replace every 4 oz of meat with a quarter of a cup of lentils when following the recipe.

Salad

Cooked lentils are lovely added to salads! They give extra crunch and flavor to just about any salad and taste especially good with curried egg, feta cheese, tomato, onion; you name it!

Soup

Lentils are a great filler for any soup! A handful of lentils thrown in with your usual recipe will give your soup extra texture and protein, not to mention flavor. Lentils are a handy thickener in soups and stews too! You do need to watch that you have enough liquid so it doesn't boil dry, the soup is stirred regularly so you don't burn the bottom and the soup is allowed to simmer for at least 10-20 minutes so that the lentils are soft.

Sophie's red lentil bolognaise

You can use lentils to make just about any meat dish go further. Use them to bulk out ground beef dishes or casseroles; you can even add them to stir-fries. Jackie loves having this recipe to fall back on when her cupboards are looking bare. She also loves that her boys go crazy for this nutritious dish which is low-fat and packed full of protein, calcium, vitamin B and iron. They like it so much, they frequently request it for dinner, even when there is plenty of food in the house!

1 heaped cup uncooked red lentils

2 tbsp oil

1 onion, chopped

2 cloves garlic, chopped

2 x 14 oz cans whole tomatoes

2 tbsp tomato paste

1 tsp sugar

½ tsp stock powder (any flavor)

2 tbsp basil pesto or chopped fresh/dried herbs

Salt and pepper

Bring a large saucepan of water to the boil. Pour in the lentils and stir to ensure they are not stuck on the bottom. Boil the lentils for 8-10 minutes until soft. Heat the oil in a small pan and sauté the onion and garlic until soft. In a food processor place the tomatoes, tomato paste, cooked onion and garlic, sugar, stock powder, pesto and salt and pepper. Pulse to combine. (If you do not have a processor then chop the tomatoes and combine all the ingredients in a bowl.) Drain the lentils and add to the mixture. Adjust seasoning to taste and serve over pasta or rice, accompanied by a fresh salad.

RECIPE COURTESY OF SOPHIE GRAY, DESTITUTEGOURMET.COM

Nuts

Packed full of protein, vitamins and 'healthy fats', nuts are a handy addition to any pantry. Unfortunately they have a tendency to sit on the shelf unused for ages! If you have some nuts lurking in your pantry, now is the time to find a way to use them up. As well as making convenient snacks, they are excellent companions to fruit or cheese for dessert.

Curries

Nuts are fantastic in curries. Try adding almonds, cashews or peanuts to your favorite curry recipe. Simply toast on a tray in the oven at 400F for a few minutes before scattering over the top of your cooked dish.

Nut butter

You can use pretty much any kind of nut to make butter, not just peanuts! This recipe for nut butter makes about one cup and gives you a lovely spread for sandwiches in next to no time.

2 cups toasted unsalted almonds (or you can use pecans, walnuts, cashews – whatever you have)

3-6 tbsp safflower or vegetable oil

1 tsp salt

Put the nuts and salt in a blender or food processor along with half the oil. Puree to desired consistency, adding more oil if necessary. Store in sealed, airtight jars.

Salads

Nuts are yummy in salads! Use pine nuts, pecans and walnuts to add crunch and flavor to everyday salads. They are also nice added to rice salads or even coleslaw.

Spicy snack

For a speedy snack with plenty of zing, add half a teaspoon of curry powder per cup of salted nuts. Place together in a resealable bag and shake well so that the nuts are well coated. Store in the bag or serve in small bowls for the family to nibble on whenever they like!

Stewed fruit

Nuts are great added to any stewed fruit. As well as adding extra crunch and flavor, they also add protein which makes the fruit more filling.

Stir-fries

Nuts are so good in a stir-fry. The trick to keeping them crunchy is to cook the whole stir-fry and take it out of the pan. While the pan is still hot, throw the nuts in with a bit of oil and lightly pan-fry them. Dish up everyone's meal and sprinkle your lightly fried nuts on top. Tastes and looks good!

Mushrooms

Mushrooms put the fun in fungus! With their robust taste and texture, they're known as meat for vegetarians and combine well with lots of different ingredients. Fresh, canned or dried, here are some ways you can use them up.

Creamy mushrooms

This easy stove top sauce is such a versatile way to enjoy mushrooms. Serve as part of your main meal, pop in a pie, ladle over baked potatoes or you can even serve on toast for breakfast!

> *2 tbsp butter*
> *Handful or 2 of sliced mushrooms (or 1 can)*
> *3 tbsp all-purpose flour*
> *1 cup milk*
> *Salt and pepper*

Melt the butter in a saucepan over medium heat. Add your sliced mushrooms and cook, stirring for a few minutes until soft. Mix in the flour and cook, stirring for 1 minute. Add the milk, a little at a time, stirring well with each addition. Reduce heat and keep stirring until the sauce boils and thickens. Season with salt and pepper to taste.

Gorgeous mushroom gravy

Mushrooms make a wonderful gravy for roast meats. Add canned or dried mushrooms to slow-cooked roast beef in the crockpot, along with a package of onion soup mix. What a difference!

Garlic mushrooms

They taste fantastic and sound fancy but garlic mushrooms are so easy to make. Simply slice your mushrooms and pop them in a saucepan with a tablespoon of butter or margarine and a teaspoon of crushed garlic (or one whole clove, crushed). Heat the pan over a medium heat and sauté the mushrooms gently for around five minutes until tender. Serve as a vegetable side dish or our favorite; on top of baked potatoes!

Ground beef dishes

You can add sliced mushrooms to all sorts of ground beef dishes for extra flavor (and make the dish go that little bit further). Try adding them to chili con carne, spaghetti bolognaise or lasagna to name a few. Or use them to make beef and mushroom pies, yum!

Soups and casseroles

You can add mushrooms to all kinds of soups, especially mushroom soup of course! Mushrooms are also delicious added to just about any beef or chicken casserole.

Stir-fries

One of the fastest vegetables to cook, mushrooms are an ideal ingredient in any stir-fried dish. Simply slice and throw them in your wok or pan towards the end of cooking. Easy!

Oats

These little flakes are full of healthy goodness so don't save them for breakfasts only! Try some of these handy ways to use up the oats in your cupboard.

ANZAC biscuits

Oats are an essential ingredient in ANZAC biscuits. These cookies are delicious, nutritious, long lasting and egg-free, which make them ideal for a Challenge week. Go to page 185 for the recipe.

Homemade muesli

Making your own muesli is a great way to use up all the oats, other nuts, seeds or dried fruit in your cupboard. You need a large, clean and dry storage container to make this recipe.

⅓ cup honey

4 cups rolled oats (not instant)

1 cup seeds (if you have them)

1 cup dried coconut (shredded is nice, but any kind)

2 cups dried fruit (golden raisins, apricots, whatever you have)

1 cup chopped or flaked nuts (again, whatever you have)

3 tbsp oil

Turn your oven on to 320F to warm up. Line 2 cookie trays with baking paper for later. Put all your dry ingredients in a bowl and mix together well. Melt the oil and honey together in a cup or jug in the microwave in 10 second bursts. Stir together and drizzle over the dry ingredients.

Lay out the mixture on the cookie trays and pop in the oven for 30 minutes or until golden brown. Turn the oven off and open the oven door. When the muesli is cold enough to touch, lift up your baking paper at either end and pour the muesli into the container.

Meatballs and meatloaf

Make meatballs go further while adding texture and flavor by adding a cup of oats to your usual ground beef mixture. Oats also make a great topping for meatloaf. Simply mix two tablespoons of oats in a small bowl with two tablespoons of brown sugar and one tablespoon of ketchup. Spread across the top of your prepared meatloaf and bake in the oven as usual. Tastes so good!

Oatmeal

There's no need to buy oatmeal if you have rolled oats in the house! Simply use them to make oatmeal by blitzing in a food processor.

Smoothies

For an extra healthy boost, add a few tablespoons of oats to your favorite smoothie. You can either add them raw or soak in a little water, milk or orange juice. Cover and leave overnight.

Topping

Oats make a lovely crunchy topping for fruit crumble. See Jackie's happy fruit crumble on page 170 to find out how.

Peanut butter

This nutritious paste of ground peanuts is not just for school lunchboxes! This versatile paste can be turned into all sorts of yummy dishes, just like these.

Peanut and vanilla cookies

Peanut butter makes wonderful cookies. Try this simple recipe:

½ cup peanut butter

1 stick butter

½ cup white sugar

½ cup brown sugar

½ tsp vanilla

1 egg

1⅓ cups self-rising flour

¼ tsp salt

Turn your oven on to 375F and grease two cookie sheets. Put your peanut butter, butter and sugars in a bowl and beat together until smooth. Add your vanilla and egg and mix well. Sift in the flour and salt. Mix all together well until the mixture resembles a soft dough. Form the dough into a ball, cover all over with plastic wrap and put in the fridge for half an hour until firm. Divide the dough into large bite-size balls and pop them onto the greased cookie sheets, leaving enough room for them to spread a little while cooking. Press the balls down gently with a fork to flatten slightly. Bake for 10-15 minutes until golden brown.

Sailboat snacks

Make a yummy snack that looks like a sailboat! All you need is peanut butter and some carrot and celery sticks. Cut celery sticks into 8-10cm pieces. Spread peanut butter in the groove of each celery segment. Pop the carrot sticks upright into the peanut butter for the sailboat masts.

Chili and ginger peanut sauce

This spicy peanut sauce is delicious with pasta, chicken, fish, whatever you like! So easy too – simply mix ingredients in a bowl:

¼ cup peanut butter

¼ cup plain yogurt

1 tbsp soy sauce

1 tbsp sugar

¼ tsp chili

½ tsp ground ginger

1 tbsp hot water

Mix all together until smooth. Add to cooked meat or vegetables and heat through until piping hot.

Soup

Yes, peanut soup! Easy to make and so warming. Melt two tablespoons of butter in a saucepan. Add one diced celery stick and half a grated onion. Simmer gently for around five minutes, then remove from heat. Add two tablespoons of all-purpose flour and stir in until blended. Stir in three cups of chicken stock and return to the heat for 30 minutes. Stir in half a cup of peanut butter, half a teaspoon of salt and two tablespoons of lemon juice until well combined. Serve garnished with chopped peanuts!

Pesto

Pesto! This amazing fragrant blend of basil and pine nuts is super delicious but often doesn't make it out of the fridge! Set your pesto free with some of these yummy suggestions!

Drizzle it

If your pesto is too thick to drizzle, simply stir in a little olive oil. Serve over grilled meat, vegetables, pizza, baked potatoes or burgers.

Mix and spread it

You can mix pesto with just about anything! Blend it with olive oil, mayonnaise or plain yogurt to make a fabulous salad dressing that is equally good on pasta salads and gourmet green leaf salads. Spread a little on a sandwich for a great flavor burst, or stir pesto into rice or mashed potatoes for extra color and flavor.

Pasta sauce

For the easiest pasta sauce ever, stir a tablespoon or two of pesto into cooked pasta and enjoy. If you have the ingredients on hand, try adding one cup of cooked pumpkin, half a cup of cream and toasted pine nuts.

Pastry wheels

To make these you need a sheet of puff pastry. Preheat your oven to 400F. Dot pesto evenly over the pastry sheet and sprinkle with sun-dried tomatoes. Starting with one long edge, roll the pastry up tightly like a Swiss roll, then slice into thin rounds. Place on non-stick baking sheets and cover with foil. Bake for 15 minutes then uncover and bake for 3-5 minutes more until cooked, crisp and golden.

Soup

When used as an ingredient, soup can transform an everyday meal into something terrific. Use canned, leftover or frozen soup to create an entire new meal. Jackie uses a can of condensed vegetable soup as the magic ingredient when making shepherd's pie. Everyone loves it but nobody knows the secret ingredient, until now! Try it, you'll love it too!

Casseroles

Almost any soup can be used in this **rich and creamy chicken casserole**. Simply chop up an onion and whatever chicken you have on hand. Chop up some extra vegetables too, e.g. carrot or celery. Lightly brown the onion and chicken in a frypan, then place in a casserole dish. Add your can of soup and other vegetables if using. Cover with foil or a lid and cook at 350F for one hour. Serve over cooked rice or pasta.

Lasagna

Vegetable soup puts the 'Mamma Mia!' into lasagna. Layer the ground beef and lasagna noodles as usual but instead of the béchamel (white) sauce, pour over a can of undiluted soup. It blends beautifully with the pasta and ground beef and adds a whole new layer of flavor.

Meatloaf

For the best meatloaf ever, add a can of soup! Tomato or meat-based soups work best but any flavor will do. Simply add to your usual meatloaf recipe for a tasty change everyone will love.

Muffins

Sweeter soups, such as pumpkin soup, make marvelous muffins, scones, fancy breads or fritters. The only limit is your imagination!

Potato bakes

Soup does wonders for potato bakes and just about any flavor will do. For terrific results, layer thinly sliced potatoes, plus any other vegetables you want to use up, in a shallow dish. Pour canned soup over the vegetables and top with breadcrumbs and grated cheese. Sprinkle with a little paprika or black pepper and cook at 350F for 60 minutes until golden brown and the potatoes are cooked through.

Quiches

Canned soup adds wonderful flavor to quiches. When making your usual quiche recipe, simply use in place of the usual cream or milk and enjoy the difference!

Shepherd's pie

Make your Shepherd's pie as tasty as Jackie's by adding a can of condensed vegetable soup. Brown your ground beef and diced onion, then add your can of soup (important that it's condensed soup as you don't want your mixture too runny or your potato to sink!) and a beef stock cube. Simply cook as usual and top with cooked, mashed potato.

Sour cream

Sour cream is divine! So rich, smooth and creamy – but how often do you use the whole pot? All too often half the tub gets left in the fridge to go hard and eventually gets thrown away. What a crime! Fortunately these ideas will help you to use up every last scrape.

Baking

Sour cream adds real richness and flavor to baked products. It works wonderfully in cakes and can even replace some of the fat and milk in recipes such as pancakes and cookies.

Creamy vegetables

Use sour cream to jazz up plain steamed veggies. Cook your vegetables as usual. Mix a little sour cream with an equal amount of vegetable or chicken stock, stir through a sprinkling of grated cheese and pour over the cooked veggies for a tasty dish.

Dips

You can make all kinds of yummy dips using sour cream including:

French onion dip: most supermarkets sell prepared French onion dip, but it is easy-peasy to make your own. Simply add one package of onion soup mix to a carton of sour cream, stir, and chill before serving.

Vegetable dip: mix one container of sour cream with one package of vegetable soup mix. Chill for several hours before serving if possible. Delicious with fresh veggie sticks, potato chips or crackers.

Spinach dip: Mix one tub of sour cream with 5 oz of natural yogurt (you can even use an equivalent quantity of mayonnaise if you are feeling decadent). Add one cup of cooked, chopped spinach (well drained). Stir in a pinch of nutmeg and refrigerate until well chilled.

Mashed potato

Simply boil and mash your potatoes as usual, then stir in a generous blob of sour cream until well combined. How much you put in is up to you! Season to taste with salt and pepper.

Potato salad

Why buy potato salad at the deli counter when you can make it at home? Just peel and chop your potatoes into bite-size pieces and cook until just tender (you don't want them to turn to mash!). Drain well and leave to cool before stirring through enough sour cream to coat them well. Add a couple of tablespoons of chopped chives for extra color and flavor.

Sauces

Sour cream can be added to most dishes in place of cream for a lovely decadent flavor. You can also transform a tomato-based sauce with a dash of sour cream.

Soups

Pumpkin soup just isn't pumpkin soup without a comforting blob of sour cream floating on the top! Add a tablespoon of sour cream to your favorite soup as a final touch just before serving and enjoy the difference.

Sweet potato (kumara)

You can pick up sweet potato for as little as $1 per two pounds in season, so it's great for your $21 Challenge week – but what can you do with it? The general rule with sweet potato is you can substitute it one for one in any potato or pumpkin recipe. For example, if a recipe calls for two medium potatoes (10 oz) you can swap them for an equal amount of sweet potato. Here are some simple examples:

Mashed

Peel and dice the sweet potato and cook in a large pan of boiling water for 20 minutes. Drain all the water, then mash the sweet potatoes well with plenty of butter, a good splash of milk and a sprinkling of salt or ground nutmeg. Sweet potato can take a little longer to cook than regular potato so keep an eye on them and test with a fork until they are tender and break up easily.

Pie topping

Sweet potato makes a delicious 'potato top' for a shepherd's pie and goes especially well on top of a smoked fish pie. Simply cook and mash sweet potato as usual before spreading on top of your filling and baking at 350F for around 20 minutes until the potato is crisp and golden.

Potato bake

Yet another delicious way to cook sweet potato! Just swap your regular potato for sweet potato when making your favorite potato bake recipe.

Roasted

You can roast sweet potato just like you would a piece of pumpkin. This recipe for roasted veggies is delicious and so versatile. Get creative and use whichever veggies, herbs or spices you have on hand. Turn your oven on to 350-400F to heat up. Peel and chop up your vegetables for roasting. Simply spread them on a cookie pan and coat with a little oil. For something a little fancier pop them in a plastic bag with a tablespoon of oil, a pinch of herbs (rosemary or thyme work well), some crushed garlic and salt. Shake the bag vigorously so all the vegetables are covered, then lay them on a cookie pan. Roast in the oven for around 50 minutes.

Soups

You can add sweet potato to just about any soup recipe. They are particularly nice in curry-based soups. Simply peel and chop and use as well as, or in place of, regular potato.

Wedges

Sweet potato wedges are a great way to get younger family members to eat sweet potato! First set your oven to 400F to heat up while you're preparing the sweet potatoes. Peel the sweet potatoes and cut into chunky wedges. Put three tablespoons of oil in a bowl and put the wedges in the bowl, mixing around vigorously until all the wedges are coated with the oil. Tip onto a large cookie pan or roasting dish and cook for 30 minutes in the oven, turning once. Eat just as you would normal potato wedges, either on their own or as a vegetable accompaniment to your main meat dish.

Sun-dried tomatoes

Sun-dried tomatoes have a wonderful concentrated flavor, so a little goes a long way. They're high in antioxidants and vitamin C, low on sodium and fat and have an unfortunate habit of getting lost in the fridge or pantry. Get them out and use them up!

Omelette

Add a touch of class to your next omelette by throwing in a handful of sun-dried tomatoes. An awesome color and taste combination!

Pasta

You can add sun-dried tomatoes to all sorts of pasta dishes, but this speedy recipe is Jackie's absolute favorite! You can make as little or as much as you like. Put some hot, cooked pasta in a bowl. Stir through one tablespoon of pesto. Chop half a cup of sun-dried tomatoes, add to the pasta and mix well. Crumble some feta cheese over the top and stir gently to combine. Out of this world! You can even add a handful of toasted pine nuts if you like, but it's just as good without.

Pastry parcels

You can use filo or puff pastry to make these delightfully flavorsome parcels. Simply mix some crumbled feta or ricotta cheese in a bowl with your sun-dried tomatoes. Cut each pastry sheet into quarters and place a portion of the mixture into each quarter. Bring the corners together and pinch or twist the edges to seal the individual parcels before baking in the oven at 350F until crisp and golden.

Pizza

Don't be tempted by take out! Sun-dried tomatoes taste fantastic on top of every pizza. Pizzas are a fabulous meal that can be made in minutes, especially if you cheat by following our recipe on page 265.

Salads

Sun-dried tomatoes are brilliant in salads! You can use them to brighten up a green salad, or add extra bite to potato or pasta salads just to name a few. Add them to cooked green beans for a tasty change.

Spread

Mix sun-dried tomatoes with cream cheese and spread on crackers.

Toasted sandwiches

Add a gourmet touch to the humble toasted sandwich by adding sun-dried tomatoes. Particularly good with cheese and onion!

Sweet chili sauce

Is it just us, or does everyone have a bottle of sweet chili sauce sitting in their fridge that they never really know quite what to do with? If this sounds like you, try some of these handy tricks to jazz up your meals with sweet chili sauce. Liquid gold in a bottle!

Burgers

Add zing to burgers by drizzling sweet chili sauce over the meat before popping the top on the bun. It's out of this world in chicken burgers!

Dip

If you have a tub of cream cheese and a bottle of sweet chili sauce in your fridge, you have a tasty dip in seconds. Just tip the cream cheese into a bowl, pour three to four tablespoons of sweet chili sauce on top and mash it in until well combined. You can also mix one whole avocado with two tablespoons of sour cream and two tablespoons of sweet chili sauce for a guacamole variation.

Marinade

For a delicious Asian-style marinade, mix one cup of sweet chili sauce with one teaspoon of crushed garlic, half a teaspoon of ginger, the zest of one orange and two tablespoons of orange juice. Use to marinate meat, or on its own as a tangy dipping sauce.

Potato wedges

Dress up a bowl of plain potato wedges by drizzling with sweet chili sauce. If you want to be really decadent, finish with a sprinking of grated cheese and top with a great big dollop of sour cream. YUM!

Satay

To make satay sauce with plenty of zing, put one teaspoon of oil, two cloves of crushed garlic and two teaspoons of grated ginger in a saucepan. Add one cup of chicken stock, one cup of coconut milk, two tablespoons of peanut butter, two tablespoons of soy sauce and two tablespoons of sweet chili sauce. Mix well and heat ingredients through until piping hot.

Tahini

Tahini paste is high in calcium and vitamin E. It is made by grinding up sesame seeds and is very good for you! Unfortunately many of us have no idea what it is, let alone what to do with it.

Breakfast

Spread tahini on toast and top with slices of cheese. A very tasty and healthy way to start the day!

Dip

Tahini is a key ingredient in a variety of Middle Eastern dips such as hummus on page 201 and baba ganoush on page 222.

Salad dressing

You can use tahini to make a yummy yogurt salad dressing. Combine two tablespoons of yogurt, a quarter of a teaspoon of salt, one tablespoon of vinegar, and one teaspoon of tahini paste in a screw-top jar and give it a good shake.

Smoothies

Tahini makes your average smoothie incredibly tasty and filling. Add one tablespoon of tahini paste per serving to your favorite smoothie combo for a nutritious boost.

Toast

Tahini and honey on toast is a very tasty and healthy way to start the day!

Stir-fries

Jazz up your stir-fries with tahini. Fiona's favorite stir-fry is made from fresh sliced vegetables tossed with thin slices of meat, two cloves of crushed garlic, two tablespoons of honey and one tablespoon of tahini. Delicious, filling and so good for you!

Fiona's gluten and dairy-free veggie patties

No meat in the freezer? No problem! These healthy vegetable patties are fast, filling and packed with flavor.

1 large carrot, peeled and grated

1 large zucchini, grated

4 cloves crushed garlic

1 tsp each paprika and ground cumin

1 tsp salt

1 tbsp tahini paste

½ cup rice flour

1 egg

Mix your carrot, zucchini, garlic, paprika, cumin, salt and tahini together in a large microwave proof bowl. Put your frypan on to medium heat to warm up. Place your bowl of ingredients in the microwave and zap on high for one minute, then give it a good stir and zap for another minute. Remove from the microwave, stir well, then add your egg and rice flour. Mix until well combined. Pour a little oil into your preheated frypan. Scoop a heaped tablespoon of the mixture into the pan and flatten it out with the back of the spoon. Keep going until the pan is full. Cook the patties for a few minutes until the underside is golden and 'done', then turn them over and cook the other side. Repeat the process until all of the mixture is used and the patties are crisp and golden brown.

Tomatoes (canned)

One of the most common ingredients people seem to unearth when doing their $21 Challenge inventories are lots of cans of tomatoes. We have no idea how they just seem to accumulate – but we DO have some great ideas for using them up. If you've got a can of tomatoes, you're never far from a meal!

Breakfast

Canned tomatoes are delicious served warm or cold for breakfast. Enjoy them hot over slices of toast or with bacon and eggs.

Curries and casseroles

Canned tomatoes make fantastic curries and casseroles so get those recipe books out or get online and see what you can find. Kate's thymely tomato casserole on page 138 is a great family meal.

Pizza sauce

For authentic tasting pizza sauce place crushed garlic and oil in a pan and cook lightly. Add canned tomatoes (squash them down as you go), fresh basil, salt and pepper. Cook over a medium heat until they break down. Strain out the basil and any larger chunks and you are ready to go! It freezes well, so make extra if you can.

Speedy side dish

Slice a couple of zucchini into a microwave-proof bowl. Pour over one 14 oz can of tomatoes. Sprinkle with black pepper and stir to combine. Microwave on high for five minutes. Terrific with steak or chicken.

Jackie's potato tauli

Jackie's family loves tauli! This recipe from her trusty childhood *The Blue Peter Book of Gorgeous Grub* is a favorite. Not only is it a great way to use up canned tomatoes, you can adapt the recipe to include any other vegetables you have on hand, such as celery, pumpkin or sweet potato. This makes a filling vegetarian dish on its own or to accompany meat.

2 onions, chopped

6 tbsp butter or margarine

1 x 14 oz can tomatoes

2 carrots, peeled and diced

2 lb potatoes, peeled and diced

Salt and pepper to taste

Melt the butter in a saucepan over medium heat. Add the onions and cook, stirring until golden (don't let them burn). Add your tomatoes and carrots, cover and cook for 30 minutes. Add the potatoes and plenty of salt and pepper. Cover and cook on low heat, stirring frequently to prevent burning for a further 30-40 minutes or until the vegetables are tender. If you like a hot dish, you can add a pinch of paprika or a dash of Worcestershire sauce 10 minutes before serving.

For more ways to use up canned tomatoes,
don't forget to check out these recipes too!

Jackie's 'save the planet' soup – Luscious lunches – Page 121
Star Wars hotpot – Divine dinners – Page 142
Kate's thymely tomato casserole – Divine dinners – Page 138
Kate's lifesaving beef – Kid-friendly food – Page 162
Sophie's red lentil bolognaise – Bonus meals – Page 230

Wheat germ

It looks a bit like sawdust and most people have no idea what to do with it! However, it's well worth finding out. Wheat germ is packed with essential nutrients, making it one of the healthiest ingredients in your pantry. Wheat germ is the site of nourishment for the growing wheat plant. In the milling of white flour the germ, rich in B vitamins and protein, is removed. Fortunately you can find it in the cereal aisle of your supermarket. A huge bonus with wheat germ is that you can hide it in all sorts of places – in smoothies, bread mixes or on cereal. Who would have thought!

Banana snack

For a healthy snack, peel and slice a banana, toast some wheat germ (see instructions on the next page) and place in a bowl. Then dip banana slices in honey or milk, roll in the wheat germ and serve.

Cereal topper

Boost your morning meal by sprinkling a quarter of a cup of wheat germ over your favorite breakfast cereal. Especially good with muesli!

Crumb coating

Add a quarter cup of wheat germ to every one cup of flour or breadcrumbs when coating meat, fish, poultry or vegetables, or when making crumb topping. Roll meat or fish in the crumb mix to cover before pan frying as usual.

Nutritious baking

Adding wheat germ to everyday bread, muffin and cookie recipes is a great way to sneak in some extra nutrition. Replace one quarter of the recipes' flour with wheat germ (add a touch of baking powder if using self-rising flour). You will soon have whittled down your stash and made some extra space on your pantry shelf.

Savory topping

Add pizzazz to your pizza topping by mixing wheat germ with grated cheese. You can even use this as a topping on oven baked dishes.

Smoothie

Raw wheat germ is healthier than cooked wheat germ. Supplement your breakfast milkshake or smoothie with some wheat germ in the blender. Simply make your favorite smoothie as usual and add a quarter cup of wheat germ for every one cup of smoothie. Sprinkle an extra one or two teaspoons of wheat germ on top before serving if liked.

Toasted wheat germ

You can use toasted wheat germ in all sorts of tasty ways. To toast your own, spread a quarter of a cup of raw wheat germ on a baking sheet. Bake at 350F for about five minutes. Once cooked, enjoy as a crunchy topping on salads, sprinkled on top of your favorite yogurt, ice cream, or even added to casseroles.

Zucchini

The humble zucchini is often found withering away at the back of the fridge. This is a huge shame because there are so many things you can do with it! You can steam it for a snack, use it as a filler in stir-fry, make savory fritters or even sneak it into chocolate cake for extra vitamins.

BBQ

Zucchini make a lovely side dish at a BBQ. You can cut it in half lengthways and fry it next to your sausages. Or, if you want some real 'bite', mix a teaspoon of chili powder with a tablespoon of 'good' oil and a couple of cloves of crushed garlic. Stir well to blend the ingredients, then drizzle over the zucchini as they cook.

Cakes

You will be amazed where you can hide a zucchini! Naomi hides a cup of zucchini in all kinds of homemade chocolate cake recipes. Her kids have never been the wiser – or even the adults that she's served it to! Just grate the whole zucchini – skin and all – and add it to your cake mix. It will make it lovely and moist and much healthier for a treat.

Quick microwave snack

For a really quick snack, slice a zucchini in half lenthways and microwave for about 30 seconds. Spread butter on top, let it melt and enjoy!

Quiche, slices and frittatas

Zucchini is excellent grated into egg-based dishes. The most popular of these is zucchini slice which has the added advantage of being super versatile – it is excellent for breakfast, lunch or dinner! You can find plenty of great recipes online.

Soup

This is Jackie's all time favorite zucchini soup. She loves it because it's so fast to make and is a great way to use up zucchini. Even if you're not a zucchini lover we recommend you try it! This fantastic recipe shows just how easy it is to turn a few basic ingredients into something incredible.

2 tsp butter or oil

1 lb zucchini, unpeeled and finely sliced

2 cups chicken stock (homemade or mixed from powder)

⅓ cup cream (or you can use milk)

1 small onion, peeled and chopped

1 medium potato, peeled and finely diced

Salt and pepper to taste

Heat butter or oil over medium heat in a large saucepan. Add onion and cook for a few minutes, then add your sliced zucchini. Add your potato, chicken stock and seasoning and simmer over a low heat for about 15 minutes until soft. Puree in a food processor or with a stick blender. When ready to serve, reheat and stir in the cream or milk.

Stir-fry

Zucchini can go in just about any stir-fry. Just grate, slice or dice and add to the pan shortly before the end of cooking.

Part 7

How to save a meal –
substituting ingredients

There's nothing worse than being mid-way through a recipe and finding you're missing a vital ingredient – particularly during a $21 Challenge week! However, there's no need to despair or rush off to the store; many ingredients can be substituted with next to no fuss or cost. Here is a comprehensive list of some handy substitutes you may be happy to call on when 'making do' with what you already have in your pantry. We have also added a 'fast find' at the end so you can get the information you need in a hurry while you are cooking. We hope you find this section as helpful as we already have!

Baking powder

Baking powder helps food rise and is used in cakes, quick breads, pancakes and cookies. It's a combination of baking soda and an acid, such as cream of tartar (tartaric acid).

To make your own baking powder mix two parts cream of tartar with one part baking soda (in Australia we call baking soda, bicarb soda).

Breadcrumbs

You can substitute all sorts of things for breadcrumbs, many of which result in some fantastic flavors! Try ground cornflakes, rolled oats or other breakfast cereals, savory cookies or crackers, pretzels, potato chips or coconut to name a few.

To make your own breadcrumbs, blitz three or four slices of torn bread for a few seconds in a blender or food processor. You can use the crust ends from a loaf of bread or even bread rolls.

A great gluten-free substitute for breadcrumbs is crushed rice cereals such as Rice Krispies. You'll hardly taste the difference! Just be sure to check the pack for the gluten-free statement.

Brown sugar

Brown sugar is simply white sugar and molasses combined. To make your own light brown sugar, combine one cup white sugar with one tablespoon of molasses, maple syrup or honey.

Butter

You can generally replace butter with the same quantity of margarine, vegetable oil or shortening.

Buttermilk

Buttermilk is a popular choice when making scones, cookies, pikelets and pancakes because of its tangy, acidic flavor. Buttermilk can be replaced by adding two teaspoons of lemon juice or vinegar to one cup milk. Let stand for five minutes.

If you don't have any milk at all, you could use sour cream or yogurt.

Cocoa and chocolate chips

Why is cocoa so-called when it originates from the cacao bean? For no more reason than an age-old spelling mistake! Fortunately it tastes heavenly however you spell it. You can replace 6 oz milk chocolate bits with half a cup of cocoa, half a cup of sugar and half a cup of shortening.

Dark chocolate

Dark chocolate is usually made up of 70% cocoa and is not as sweet as milk chocolate. You can get a pretty good match by using a quarter of a cup of cocoa (or carob powder) and one tablespoon of butter for each ounce of dark chocolate.

Chocolate bar

Yes, it is actually possible to include an entire chocolate bar in your cooking, even if you don't have one! You can replace one 4 oz chocolate bar with a quarter of a cup of cocoa, a third of a cup of sugar and three tablespoons of shortening.

Cornstarch

Cornstarch can be made from either corn (maize) or wheat. This super soft powder is used to thicken sauces, gravies, pie fillings and puddings. You can replace one tablespoon of cornstarch with one and a half tablespoons of flour or arrowroot powder for a similar result. If the purpose is to thicken a soup or stew, try adding grated potato instead.

Cream

You can replace one cup of cream with three quarters of a cup of milk and one quarter of a cup of butter, or one cup of evaporated milk, or a blend of equal parts milk and cottage cheese.

Today's popular low-fat substitutes like lite cream or evaporated milk tend to separate or curdle when added to sauces. To prevent this from happening put the lite cream or evaporated milk in a saucepan and reduce it lightly over a low heat before adding it to your cooking. Don't let it boil. If you find your sauce is too thin, simply thicken it by adding cornstarch and then heating it gently as if you are making a white sauce.

Cream of tartar (tartaric acid)

Cream of tartar is a white crystalline powder. Its main purpose is to act as a leavening agent. You can replace half a teaspoon of cream of tartar with one and a half teaspoons of lemon juice or vinegar.

Eggs

We all know where eggs come from but we don't always have them when we need them! Next time you get stuck, try some of these easy substitutes for eggs. Each 'makes' the equivalent of one egg:

2 tbsp cornstarch

2 tbsp arrowroot flour

2 tbsp potato starch

1 heaped tbsp soy powder and 2 tbsp water

1 tbsp soy milk powder, 1 tbsp cornstarch and 2 tbsp water

1 mashed banana or ½ cup apple sauce can be substituted in cakes or muffins

When breading meat or chicken and you have run out of egg, half a cup of yogurt, sour cream or mayonnaise will coat about four to six pieces of meat or chicken.

Garlic

Garlic is used in all sorts of dishes, which is terrific as it's so good for you. But if you don't happen to have any when a recipe calls for it, don't panic!

One eighth of a teaspoon of garlic powder is equivalent to one small garlic clove, and one teaspoon of crushed garlic is equivalent to one garlic clove.

Other substitutes include garlic powder and garlic flakes, using half a teaspoon of garlic flakes for every clove of garlic. Garlic salt can be substituted by using half a teaspoon of garlic salt for every clove of fresh garlic. Remember to reduce added salt if called for in the recipe. Onions, green onions, garlic chives and French shallots all make good substitutes too.

Gelatin

If a recipe calls for powdered gelatin and you only have leaves on hand (or vice versa), just remember three teaspoons of powdered gelatin is equal to six gelatin leaves.

Herbs (fresh and dried)

If you don't have the right herb for a particular recipe, no problem – any of the following will do instead. These suggestions are suitable for both fresh and dried herbs. While the flavor may not be as originally intended in the recipe, the result will still be delicious and nobody else will know!

When a recipe calls for fresh herbs and you only have dried, simply use half to one teaspoon of dried herbs for every one tablespoon of fresh herbs.

Herb substitutions

Basil:	Oregano or thyme
Chervil:	Tarragon or parsley
Chives:	Green onion, onion or even leek
Marjoram:	Basil or thyme
Mint:	Basil, thyme or rosemary
Oregano:	Basil or thyme
Rosemary:	Thyme or tarragon
Sage:	Marjoram or rosemary
Thyme:	Basil, marjoram or oregano

Honey

There are over 300 kinds of honey! Even if you don't have one of them in your pantry, you can come up with some pretty close substitutes. Try replacing honey with maple syrup or brown rice syrup. It won't be as sweet so you could always add a little sugar.

Lemon juice

The best way to make sure you never run out of lemons is to plant a tree in your backyard! Until you do, you can replace one teaspoon of lemon juice with half a teaspoon of vinegar or grapefruit or lime juice.

Milk

You can use milk fresh, powdered, canned or UHT. An easy substitute for one cup of milk is to mix half a cup of evaporated milk with one cup water.

Nuts and seeds

No, we haven't gone nuts; you really can substitute different nuts in recipes if you need to! You can:

- replace macadamia nuts with almonds or hazelnuts and vice versa

- use cashews in place of pine nuts

- switch poppy seeds with sesame seeds

- replace pumpkin seeds with finely chopped almonds, peanuts or cashews.

If it's the nutty texture you're after, you could even try using toasted oatmeal or Rice Krispies. Hazelnut and almond meal can also impart a nutty flavor in baking. However, if you want the nuts to sweeten a recipe (such as in carrot cake) you can also substitute them with canned pineapple.

Palm sugar

Palm sugar is mainly used in Asian cooking. You can replace it with brown sugar.

Pizza crusts

You don't need pizza crusts to make pizza. Instead, you can make 'Cheat's Pizza' by swapping the crust for toast, half a bread roll, English muffins or pita bread. Simply throw everything together as if you were making a pizza. Spread your base with tomato paste or ketchup. Sprinkle with herbs, your favorite toppings and cheese. Cook at 400F for 5-10 minutes until golden brown. Alternatively, microwave for one to two minutes – a great trick is to put a piece of paper towel underneath your toast to help prevent the bread getting soggy.

Red wine

It's not usually a good idea to replace red wine in a recipe with white wine. Red wines are heavier and much stronger in flavor. You can, however, replace half a cup of red wine with two tablespoons of sherry, port, cranberry juice, balsamic or red wine vinegar. A stout style beer may also be used in place of red wine in casseroles.

Ricotta cheese

Replace one cup of ricotta cheese with one cup of drained cottage cheese. And if you are really stuck, you can just use regular cheese!

Seafood cocktail sauce

Believe it or not, seafood cocktail sauce is easy to make! Simply mix one cup of mayonnaise, two tablespoons of ketchup and a squeeze of lemon juice. Nobody will ever know the difference.

Self-rising flour

To convert all-purpose flour to self-rising flour, add two teaspoons of baking powder to one cup of all-purpose flour. You can also use one teaspoon of cream of tartar and half a teaspoon of baking soda to one cup of all-purpose flour.

Shortening

If your recipe calls for shortening (often used in pastries) but you don't have any then you can use other types of solidified oils such as butter, lard, coconut oil or margarine.

Sour cream

If you have run out of sour cream, there's no need to give up and go to the store. Sour cream is simply cream that has had a culture added. Alternatives are UHT cream, fresh cream, cream cheese, plain yogurt, even cottage cheese at a pinch.

Spices

One of the wonderful things about spices, apart from their fantastic flavor, is that you can mix and match them where necessary. The alternatives included in the table on the next page should work with most recipes if you don't have the right spice on hand.

Sugar

Replace sugar with honey, corn syrup or some molasses. For bread making, use one cup of honey plus a pinch of baking soda. You can even make superfine sugar or confectioners sugar by putting white sugar in the blender.

Spice substitutions

Allspice: Use a little clove, nutmeg, cinnamon and pepper
                 to replace allspice, or simply mix half a teaspoon
                 of cinnamon with half a teaspoon of ground
                 cloves to make one teaspoon of allspice

Aniseed: Fennel seed or a few drops of aniseed extract

Cardamom: Ginger

Chili powder: A dash of chili sauce plus a little oregano and
                 cumin if you have it. You can also use red
                 cayenne pepper, chili flakes or hot paprika

Cinnamon: Use nutmeg or allspice, but only a quarter of the
                 amount

Cloves: Allspice, cinnamon or nutmeg

Cumin: Chili powder

Ginger: Allspice, cinnamon or nutmeg

Mace: Nutmeg

Nutmeg: Cinnamon or ginger

Saffron: You can replace saffron with a dash of turmeric
                 to add color. So much cheaper than saffron too!

Sweetened condensed milk

You can make your own sweetened condensed milk by combining one heaped cup of milk powder with half a cup of warm water and three quarters of a cup of sugar. Blend until combined, store in the fridge.

Tartar sauce

Tartar sauce is a classic accompaniment to many fish dishes. You can make your own version by mixing one tablespoon of relish with one cup of mayonnaise and two tablespoons of lemon juice.

Tomato paste

Rich and delicious, tomato paste can be found in thousands of recipes. If you don't happen to have any on hand, one peeled, deseeded and chopped tomato is equal to one tablespoon of tomato paste. Chopped, roasted red bell peppers are equally delicious if you have them, or simply replace one tablespoon of tomato paste with two to three tablespoons of tomato puree or ketchup. Store any leftover tomato paste in ice cube containers in the freezer so you'll never be caught short again.

Tomato puree

One cup of tomato puree can be replaced with two tablespoons of tomato paste blended with one cup of water or tomato juice. You could even use pasta sauce or canned tomato soup.

Vinegar

Vinegar has thousands of uses – every home should have a bottle! However, if you don't, you can replace one tablespoon of white vinegar with one tablespoon of lemon or lime juice.

Whipping cream

You can replace one cup of whipping cream with one third of a cup of melted butter and three quarters of a cup of milk. For cream-based sauces you can also try sour cream or evaporated milk.

White wine

You can replace one cup of white wine with one cup of water, three tablespoons of lemon juice and one tablespoon of sugar. You could also use three quarters of a cup of apple juice and three tablespoons of lemon juice. If you need wine for a marinade, you can use vinegar or beer instead. For salad dressings use lemon juice.

Yogurt

Substitute one cup of thick sour milk, buttermilk or sour cream for one cup of yogurt.

Yeast

If your recipe calls for fresh yeast and you only have dried yeast, just use half the specified quantity of dried yeast.

Special thanks to Tracey Galea, food technologist and Simple Savings member for helping us out with this section.

Substituting ingredients fast

Remember this table is here in case – eek – you're in the middle of cooking something wonderful and discover too late that you don't have everything you need. There's no time to spare but don't panic! We've made this super quick reference table to get you out of a tight spot in a hurry.

ingredient	amount	substitution
Allspice	1 tsp	¼ tsp each clove, nutmeg, cinnamon & pepper, *or* ½ tsp cinnamon with ½ tsp ground cloves
Aniseed	¼ tsp	¼ tsp fennel seed, *or* a few drops of aniseed extract
Baking powder	1 tsp	Mix ⅔ tsp cream of tartar and ⅓ tsp baking soda
Basil	1 tbsp	1 tbsp oregano or thyme
Breadcrumbs	1 cup	1 cup ground cornflakes, *or* 1 cup rolled oats, *or* 1 cup crushed breakfast cereals, *or* 1 cup crushed savory crackers, *or* 1 cup crushed potato chips, *or* 1 cup coconut
Brown sugar (light)	1 cup	1 cup white sugar with 1 tbsp honey *or* 1 tbsp maple syrup
Brown sugar (dark)	1 cup	1 cup white sugar with 2 tbsp honey *or* 2 tbsp maple syrup
Butter	1 cup	1 cup either margarine or vegetable oil, *or* 1 cup shortening, *or* 1 cup coconut oil

Substituting ingredients

ingredient	amount	substitution
Buttermilk	1 cup	Add 2 tsp lemon juice or vinegar to 1 cup milk and let stand for 5 minutes, *or* 1 cup either sour cream or yogurt
Cardamom	1 tsp	1 tsp ginger
Chervill	1 tbsp	1 tbsp tarragon or parsley
Chili powder	¼ tsp	⅛ tsp each oregano & cumin, dash of chili sauce
Chives	1 tbsp	1 tbsp green onion, onion or even leek
Chocolate	4 oz	¼ cup cocoa, ⅓ cup sugar and 3 tbsp shortening
Cinnamon	1 tsp	¼ tsp nutmeg or allspice
Cloves	1 tsp	1 tsp allspice, cinnamon or nutmeg
Cocoa	1 tbsp	2 tbsp chocolate drinking powder (remove 1 tbsp sugar from recipe)
Cornstarch	1 tbsp	1½ tbsp flour or arrowroot powder
Cream	1 cup	¾ cup milk and ¼ cup butter, *or* 1 cup evaporated milk, *or* a blend of equal parts milk and cottage cheese
Cream of tartar	½ tsp	1½ tsp lemon juice or vinegar, *or* ½ tsp tartaric acid
Cumin	1 tsp	1 tsp chili powder
Dark chocolate	1oz	¼ cup cocoa (or carob powder) and 1 tbsp butter

Substituting ingredients

ingredient	amount	substitution
Eggs	1 large	2 tbsp cornstarch, arrowroot flour or potato starch, *or* 1 heaped tbsp soy powder and 2 tbsp water, *or* 1 tbsp soy milk powder, 1 tbsp cornstarch and 2 tbsp water, *or* 1 mashed banana or ½ cup apple sauce can be substituted in cakes or muffins, *or* yogurt, sour cream, mayonnaise, milk or buttermilk can be substituted for eggs when breading meat or chicken
Garlic	1 clove	⅛ tsp garlic powder for 1 small garlic clove, *or* 1 tsp crushed garlic for 1 garlic clove
Gelatin	6 leaves	3 tsp powdered gelatin, *or* 1 package (⅓ oz)
Ginger	1 tsp	1 tsp allspice, cinnamon or nutmeg
Honey	1 tbsp	1 tbsp maple syrup or brown rice syrup. It won't be as sweet so you could always add a little sugar
Lemon juice	1 tsp	½ tsp vinegar or grapefruit or lime juice
Macadamia nuts	1 cup	1 cup almonds or hazelnuts
Mace	1 tsp	1 tsp nutmeg
Marjoram	1 tbsp	1 tbsp basil or thyme
Milk	1 cup	½ cup evaporated milk with 1 cup water
Mint	1 tbsp	1 tbsp basil, thyme or rosemary

Substituting ingredients

ingredient	amount	substitution
Nutmeg	1 tsp	1 tsp cinnamon or ginger
Nuts		Refer to nut and seed subsitions on page 264
Oregano	1 tbsp	1 tbsp basil or thyme
Palm sugar	1 cup	1 cup brown sugar
Pine nuts	1 cup	1 cup cashew nuts
Pizza crust	large	Pita bread, muffins, toast, bread roll or tortillas
Red wine	½ cup	2 tbsp sherry, port, balsamic vinegar, red wine vinegar or cranberry juice, *or* ½ cup stout beer for casseroles
Ricotta cheese	1 cup	1 cup drained cottage cheese, *or* 1 cup regular cheese
Rosemary	1 tbsp	1 tbsp thyme or tarragon
Saffron	A dash	Dash of turmeric to add color
Sage	1 tbsp	1 tbsp marjoram or rosemary
Seafood cocktail sauce	1 cup	1 cup mayonnaise, 2 tbsp ketchup and a squeeze of lemon juice
Self-rising flour	1 cup	Add 2 tsp baking powder to 1 cup all purpose flour, *or* 1 tsp cream of tartar and ½ tsp baking soda to 1 cup all-purpose flour
Sesame seeds	1 cup	1 cup black poppy seeds

Substituting ingredients

ingredient	amount	substitution
Shortening	1 cup	1 cup butter, coconut oil, lard or margarine
Sour cream	1 cup	1 cup fresh cream, UHT cream, cream cheese, plain yogurt or cottage cheese
Sugar	1 cup	1 cup honey or corn syrup
Sweetened condensed milk	1½ cups	Blend 1 heaped cup milk powder with ½ cup warm water and ¾ cup sugar. Store in the fridge
Tartar sauce	1 cup	1 cup mayonnaise, 1 tbsp relish and 2 tbsp lemon juice
Thyme	1 tbsp	1 tbsp basil, marjoram or oregano
Tomato paste	1 tbsp	1 peeled, deseeded and chopped tomato, *or* 2-3 tbsp tomato puree or ketchup
Tomato puree	1 cup	2 tbsp tomato paste blended with 1 cup water or tomato juice, *or* 1 cup either pasta sauce or tomato soup
Vinegar	1 tbsp	1 tbsp lemon or lime juice
Whipping cream	1 cup	⅓ cup melted butter and ¾ cup milk
White wine	1 cup	1 cup water, 3 tbsp lemon juice and 1 tbsp sugar, *or* ¾ cup apple juice and 3 tbsp lemon juice
Yeast (fresh)	1 tsp	½ tsp dried yeast to make 1 tsp of fresh
Yogurt	1 cup	1 cup thick sour milk, buttermilk or sour cream

Part 8
How did you do?

Congratulations! You have reached the end of your $21 Challenge! We hope you have had a lot of fun! We would love to hear how it went! How did you do? Did you surprise yourself? How much did you save? Write and let us know!

The next step

With the $21 Challenge you have discovered how much money you can save in a single week. Feels great, doesn't it! Now we've got you up and running, it's time for you to learn what you can REALLY do. If you want to make a start on saving LOTS more money right now, head for our website!

About the Simple Savings website

Simple Savings is a goldmine of information where you can learn how to save money on EVERY aspect of your life, not just food!

When you visit the site, you will find thousands of pages of FREE information. The site is huge and there's always so much going on that it's hard to know where to start! So to make it easier, here is a quick guide to help you:

- **Free newsletter.** The best thing to do is to sign up to our free newsletter. This will keep you up to date with the latest information. Our weekly newsletter, Hint of the Week, contains the best money saving tips sent in by members each week. Our monthly newsletters are more detailed and full of information to inspire you.

  Once you have subscribed to our free newsletters, take a peek at some of our fantastic freebies. Just click on the links to start saving!

- **Penny's Blog** is a great place to start. Jackie has been blogging her savings journey here since 2005 and some of her blogs are downright hilarious!

- **War on Debt** will take you to our free yearly planner. It is a system to help you save money and get out of debt. Simply print it out and put it up!

- **Bill Payment System** is another fantastic freebie. Use this system to organize both your bills and your budget. The Bill Payment system will help keep you on track and even help you get ahead with your bills. No complicated spreadsheets, no more late payment fees, no worries!

- **Save-O-Meter** shows you how much money you can save by changing a few habits. You'll be amazed!

   As you can see, you can learn heaps by visiting the free areas of the Simple Savings site. However the real gem is the paid area – the Savings Vault. It is both a massive, online 'Encyclopedia of Saving' and a fun club of frugals. There is always something new going on. Here are some of the things you'll find:

- **Thousands of useful tips**, which are carefully handpicked and edited to bring you the best and most reliable information.

- **A fantastic Savings Forum** where you will find thousands of likeminded, friendly people to give advice and support 24/7.

- **A 'members only' Downloads area** which features dozens of great money saving tools from spreadsheets to e-books.

- **A personalized blog area** for you to record your own money saving journey and inspire yourself and others.

   We offer a 365-day 'no questions asked' money back guarantee to join our paid members area, the Savings Vault. So give it a go!

Index

Thank you!

Just like the Simple Savings website, this book is an enormous collaboration of many brilliant, savvy minds. We wish to thank everyone for contributing. Without you, this book would not have been possible.

Thank you to Barb K, without whom the $21 Challenge would not even exist. We WILL have that drink together one day! Barb is too humble to accept the recognition she really deserves, but her resourcefulness and presence of mind has rubbed off on thousands of families and we applaud you. Thanks a million, Barb!

Thank you to all the Simple Savings members who have willingly donated their tips and recipes in these pages. Jackie and Fiona's names may be on the front cover, but you deserve the credit. This has been a massive team effort.

To the Simple Savings staff; Naomi Bruvels for holding things together, Kirstin Nicholson for her eagle eyes, Gail Crimmins for her brain, Shelley Newman, Rita Hoy and Glen Comrie for their outstanding editing.

To our brilliant, hilarious cartoonist; award winning Steve Panozzo! You can see his work every month in our Simple Savings newsletters and plenty more on his website: www.noz.com.au

To Carol, Tony, Jenny and Barry for supporting Simple Savings and helping it get to where it is today.

To Kate Andrew; thank you for lending us your sharp mind, brilliant design and cooking skills.

To Alex Craig from Pan MacMillan for her patience and advice.

To our food technologist, Tracey Galea, for help with the 'How to save a meal' section.

To Tony Deegan from Sparke Helmore for being there for us from the very beginning.

To Claire M. for all her work on the Simple Savings Forum; in particular for managing the $21 Challenge threads over the past few years. Your help and dedication on the site are outstanding!

Thank you to Marg, PJ, Suzy, Gay and Sara for their advice.

Thank you to the media. To the TV programmes, radio stations, newspapers, websites and magazines who have supported us and helped us build Simple Savings into a fantastic resource that changes people's lives. Your support has been invaluable.

And last, but definitely not least, our families who have put up with us all these months. To our husbands, Matt and Noel for the countless times they have put meals on the table because their wives were too busy writing about food to actually cook any. To our gorgeous children – Sam, Jacqui, Tristan and Elora Lippey, and Liam and Alistair Gower, all of whom have had to compete with this book for our attention. Thank you from the bottom of our hearts for your unconditional love and support.

10866221R00165

Made in the USA
Charleston, SC
11 January 2012